Science Fair Success Using Newton's Laws of Motion

Other titles in the **Science Fair Success** series

Science Fair Success

Science Fair Success Using Newton's Laws of Motion

Madeline Goodstein

Enslow Publishers, Inc.

40 Industrial Road	PO Box 38
Box 398	Aldershot
Berkeley Heights, NJ 07922	Hants GU12 6BP
USA	UK

http://www.enslow.com

Library of Congress Cataloging-in-Publication Data

Goodstein, Madeline
    Science fair success using Newton's laws of motion / Madeline Goodstein.
       p. cm. — (Science fair success)
    Includes bibliographical references and index.
    Summary: Explains concepts such as acceleration, force, friction, and gravity by using
them in simple experiments, in such real-life settings as the bowling alley and supermarket.
    ISBN 0-7660-1628-5
    1. Motion—Experiments—Juvenile literature. 2. Force and energy—Experiments—
Juvenile literature. 3. Gravity—Experiments—Juvenile literature. [1. Force and energy—
Experiments. 2. Motion—Experiments. 3. Experiments. 4. Science projects.]
I. Title. II. Series.
QC127.4 4G66   2002
531'.1'078—dc21
                                     2001003426

Printed in the United States of America

10 9 8 7 6 5 4 3 2 1

To Our Readers:
We have done our best to make sure all Internet Addresses in this book were active and
appropriate when we went to press. However, the author and the publisher have no control over
and assume no liability for the material available on those Internet sites or on other Web sites they
may link to. Any comments or suggestions can be sent by e-mail to comments@enslow.com or to
the address on the back cover.

Illustration Credits: Stephen F. Delisle

Photo Credits: © Corel Corporation, pp. 62, 94; © Hemera Technologies Inc.,
1997–2000, pp. 13, 33.

Cover Photo: Patti Sapone/The Star-Ledger.

Contents

Introduction

Following are some questions about motion for you to consider.

Why do automobile wheels spin without gripping when a car makes too fast a start?

If you need a seat belt because you are slammed forward, why do you need a headrest?

Why do some of the groceries in a shopping cart slide forward when the cart is jerked to a halt?

What makes a bowling ball curve sharply only when it gets near the pins?

If you push on a building, does it push on you?

Why doesn't the Moon fall down to Earth?

When a horse balks at a fence, refusing to go over it, what happens to the rider?

All of the questions above are answered somewhere in this book. They are answered by applying the three laws of motion stated by Isaac Newton, the seventeenth-century British scientific genius. In this book, Newton's laws of motion will be studied through a series of simple experiments. All of these experiments are easy and fun to do. Most of them take place in familiar settings: a bowling alley, a school hallway, a supermarket, or your home. The rest relate to an automobile race track and motion in outer space.

You will find that most of the materials needed for the experiments are already in your home or available in a supermarket, hardware store, or drugstore. As you carry out the

experiments, you will learn nature's secrets about motion—
secrets that were not understood for all of the centuries before
Newton explained them.

Thought Experiments

Following are three thought experiments. Each involves at
least one of the three laws of motion. Thought experiments
ask you to imagine what would happen, based upon previous
experience, if a proposed experiment were to be carried out.
They have led to some very important theories. In fact, all
three of the laws of motion proposed by Isaac Newton were
based, in part, upon thought experiments. They were thought
experiments because the conditions needed could not be
found anywhere on Earth.

In the following experiments, draw upon your own expe-
riences to find the outcome as best you can.

Experiment A

Suppose you are standing beside a perfectly smooth, level track
that runs completely around the surface of the world. You
place a perfectly round ball on the track. Then you lightly
push the ball. Do you think the ball will slow down after a little while and come to a stop? Will it instead gradually speed
up? Or will it just roll on and on at about the same speed for
a long long time, maybe even all the way around the world?

Experiment B

If you kick a ball, you can expect it to move away from you. If
you kick it harder, do you think it will go faster than before

or just go farther? How about if you kick it even harder? Is there a limit to how fast or far you can get it to go?

Experiment C

Suppose you lean on a wall. Is the wall pushing you?

The solutions to the above thought experiments may be found by applying Newton's three laws of motion as discussed in this book.

Scientific Method

All of science is based upon the scientific method. The scientific method uses experimentation and verification. Experimentation starts by wondering what would happen if a specific change were made to take place. A scientist makes a hypothesis about what would happen—his or her best guess. Then the scientist plans how to make the change occur—the experiment—to see what happens. The hypothesis is either accepted or rejected, based upon what occurs. To reach a conclusion, it is important that nothing is altered when carrying out the experiment except the one planned change. Anything else that might be able to change during the experiment—except, of course, the result—is kept under control so that it cannot vary. This is called controlling the variables. Scientists usually make additional experiments in which they increase or decrease the variable (the property that can change) or alter it in some other way to further test the hypothesis. The aim is to see whether the hypothesis can lead to a theory that predicts changes and explains how and why the changes occur.

One scientist's experiments need to be repeated by other scientists (verified) before they can be accepted. When a theory is developed, all the data obtained then and later must be consistent with the theory. If there is one piece of evidence that does not agree with the theory, the theory must be discarded or modified to account for the new evidence.

Every good theory is productive in that it leads to new ideas. Scientific progress is built upon earlier theories.

Newton's Three Laws of Motion

Isaac Newton (1642–1727), one of the most eminent scientific intellectuals of all time, was the foremost founder of modern science. He discovered the three laws of motion that present a complete analysis of motion and the rules that govern it. He also stated the law of universal gravitation, which explains the relationships between mass, distance, and gravitational force. Newton founded the sciences of optics and color, explained and predicted the paths of planets and comets, and developed calculus. A poem written by Alexander Pope in the eighteenth century sums up Sir Isaac Newton's accomplishments in these words: "Nature and God's laws lay hid in night; God said, Let Newton be! And all was light."

Newton's three laws of motion were originally published in 1687 in Latin, the language of all scholarly publications in Newton's time. The laws are listed on the next page, both in a modern version and an everyday version.

Newton's Three Laws of Motion

First Law: An object at rest will stay at rest and an object in motion will continue in motion at the same speed and in the same direction unless acted upon by another force.

Second Law: The change in speed of an object over a given time is proportional to the force exerted on it.

Third Law: Whenever a force is exerted upon an object, the object exerts an equal force back. This law is often called the law of action and reaction.

Newton's Three Laws of Motion,
Everyday Version

Below are the three laws of motion stated in terms of everyday examples.

First Law: When a car stops suddenly, the rider without a seat belt flies forward.

Second Law: A long freight train is much harder to accelerate than a Volkswagen car and, once moving, the train is much harder to stop.

Third Law: I'd rather collide with a flea than an elephant, especially if they are moving, too.

Chapter 1

Newton at the Bowling Alley

The first of Newton's three laws was built upon discoveries by Galileo Galilei (1564–1642), an Italian experimenter, astronomer, and mathematician. Before the sixteenth century, people thought that it was the nature of moving objects to slow down to a stop. It took Galileo to show otherwise. Galileo experimented with round bronze balls rolling in troughs (a trough is shaped like the gutter in a bowling alley). The ball was allowed to roll down a trough tilted downward and on to upward-tilted troughs (see Figure 1). The smoother the ball and trough, the farther up the ball would roll. However, the ball would never make it back to the starting height. Galileo knew about friction and concluded that if there were no friction, the ball would go all the way back up to the starting height. Note that Galileo could never actually roll the ball without friction. His conclusion was based on a thought experiment; that is, he carried out the final experiment in his imagination.

Galileo also found that if the upward trough was lowered a bit, the ball still rolled almost as high as before; therefore it rolled a longer upward distance. Lowering the trough more resulted in the ball going even farther. Galileo made a mental leap to the conclusion that if the ball were allowed to roll down to the floor, and if there were no friction to slow it down, it would roll around the world forever. This was a startling theory for his time. The idea that motion would

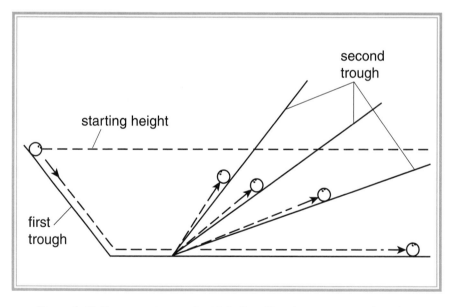

Figure 1. Galileo experimented with balls rolling down one trough and up another. The diagram shows successive lowering of the second trough. The lower the second trough, the farther the ball rolled. When the ball rolled a longer distance, it did not rise as high as before due to the additional friction. Galileo concluded that a ball that rolled down the first trough onto a horizontal surface without friction would roll on and on without stopping.

continue unchanged if there was no friction was unique. Galileo's work became the basis for Newton's first law.

Newton built upon Galileo's discovery. He mathematically described the concept of force (a push or a pull). From this he constructed a complete analysis of motion that he was even able to extend to the motion of bodies in the heavens.

In a letter dated February 5, 1676, Newton acknowledged his gratitude to those whose ideas had helped him. He wrote, "If I have seen further it is by standing on ye shoulders of Giants."

Have you ever seen an object here on Earth that just kept moving on and on at the same speed in the same direction without anything pushing or pulling it? On Earth, everything always slows down due to friction. To study Newton's three laws, it is advantageous to find a place to carry out experiments with very little friction.

There is one location available to many where this is possible. That location is a bowling alley. All bowling alleys approved by the American Bowling Congress have a very smooth, level surface, most of which is oiled. The rules say that no area on the bowling lane may be more than forty-thousandths of an inch (0.1 cm) higher or lower than any other section. The bowling ball must be smooth with the same diameter all around. All together, these requirements allow a bowling ball to follow a level, horizontal path on the lane with minimal friction. That is why many of the experiments in this chapter will take place in a bowling alley.

Each of the three laws of motion will be examined in turn.

Experiment 1.1

First Law: An Object at Rest or in Motion

Newton's first law says that an object at rest will stay at rest unless acted upon by an outside force.

Place a sturdy sheet of paper on a smooth floor. Place a bowling ball or any other heavy ball on top of the paper. Firmly grab the two corners of the paper nearest to you. Very rapidly, pull the paper horizontally toward you (see Figure 2). What happens to the bowling ball?

The bowling ball either doesn't move at all or stirs slightly. The force (pull) acts on the paper but not on the ball. According to Newton's first law, an object stays in place unless a force acts upon it. Since no force acted to move the bowling ball, it stayed in place.

Place a smooth card such as one from a playing deck on top of a drinking glass. Center a coin on top of the card. Then yank the card horizontally off the glass. What do you observe?

The coin falls into the glass. The force of your pull acts upon the card but not on the coin. The coin is left hanging in the air over the glass. The force of gravity pulls it down into the glass.

Materials

* smooth floor
* bowling ball or other heavy ball
* sturdy sheet of paper
* drinking glass
* smooth card, such as a card from deck of cards
* coin
* 2 marbles of different size
* large wok or large shallow mixing bowl

Newton's first law also says that an object in motion will continue in motion with the same speed and direction as long as it is not acted upon by an outside force.

Obtain two glass marbles of different sizes and a large wok or a mixing bowl of similar shape. Hold the marble against the inside of the wok at the top. Let go of it. Does it roll all the way down and then stop? Does it go partway or all the way to the top of the opposite side? Does it fly out of the wok? Does it roll straight back down again? Try the other marble. Is this result different? Try both marbles several times.

The marble will usually roll to the bottom and almost all the way back up. Then it will roll back down and up the other side but a little lower than before. Then it will roll back down, and so on. The size of the marble does not make any difference in the heights reached.

Figure 2. A sheet of paper is yanked out from under a heavy ball. What happens to the ball and how does this illustrate Newton's first law?

Since the marble keeps changing direction back and forth, there must be an outside force acting on it. That outside force is gravity. Gravity pulls the marble down, but the marble rolls almost all the way back up each time. It rolls back and forth, in accord with the first law, until friction finally brings it to a halt. Note that this experiment is comparable to Galileo's experiment using two connected troughs.

Experiment 1.2

First Law at the Bowling Alley

Materials

* ✱ bowling lane with bumpers in the gutters, or other location with smooth floor

* ✱ 6- to 9-lb bowling ball or substitute

* ✱ strong smooth wooden plank about 90–120 cm (3–4 ft) long and at least 20 cm (8 in) wide

* ✱ several books

* ✱ ruler

* ✱ pencil

* ✱ stopwatch or clock with second hand

If you do not have access to a bowling alley, you can use any smooth floor such as a school hall with a vinyl floor or a wooden gym floor. Do not use a carpeted floor; the friction will slow the ball down too much. Instead of a bowling ball, any smooth round ball may be used. The heavier it is, the better. Please adjust the instructions in this chapter as needed for ball and location.

Before starting, you will need to obtain permission from a bowling alley (or school, etc.) to carry out the experiment. Explain that you will be using a wooden plank to control the speed of the bowling ball for a science experiment. The plank will not touch the lane itself. Request that bumpers be placed in the gutters on both sides of the lane so as to keep the ball from falling into a gutter.

Place a smooth wooden plank on the floor at the foul line pointing down the middle of a lane. Raise the back end 10 cm (4 in) by placing books under it. Mark a line with a pencil about 15 cm (6 in) down from the top of the plank. Hold a bowling ball weighing 6 to 9 lb at the mark (see Figure 3) and release the ball to roll down into the lane. Observe. Does the ball slow down? Does it move in a straight line? Does it make it to the pins?

Lower the back end of the plank to a height of 2 cm (¾ in) by removing books as needed. Now the ball will not slide down the ramp and along the lane as rapidly as before. Place the ball at the mark and release it. Does the ball make it to the pins? Does it slow down as it moves forward?

Were you surprised to see that, at each speed, the ball rolled along the lane to the very end without a noticeable change in the speed? Even if the ball hit a side bumper, it just kept going. When the plank was barely raised, it probably looked as if the ball would never make it to the pins, but each time it did. Now you know why your little brother's or sister's ball often makes it as far as the pins even when you think the

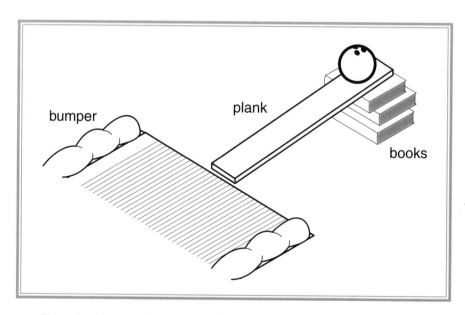

Figure 3. A bowling ball is allowed to roll straight down a wooden plank onto a bowling lane. The speed of the ball is controlled by propping up the back end of the plank, first with two books and then with one thin book. Does the ball make it to the end of the lane each time?

throw seemed too light to ever do it. This is in accord with Newton's first law, which says that the ball will keep moving in a straight line at the same speed as long as no force acts upon it. The frictional force in the lane is very small, so the ball is able to continue moving to the end.

If the ball doesn't roll in a straight line but curves instead to one of the bumpers, it may be because of the finger holes in the ball. Each time the ball rolls over a hole, you can hear it thump and see the ball slowly shift direction.

Note that for all lanes, there is no oil on the ten feet of floor in front of the pins. At that point, friction will grab the ball. It will roll, not slide, on in a straight line in the direction that it was going when it came to the unoiled portion. With a good throw, that will produce the sharp "curve" (which is really a straight line) that will carry the ball into the pins.

Project Ideas and Further Investigations

- Does a ball on a smooth, horizontal path obey Newton's first law no matter what its weight? Try bowling balls of different weights on the bowling lane and observe what happens. To make a fair comparison, you need to send each ball down the lane with the same force. You can do this by launching all the balls from the same height and angle down the plank. Consider testing other smooth balls such as a billiard ball or a hard rubber ball (always obtain permission to use the different balls on the lanes).

- Does the initial speed of a ball make a difference as to whether the ball obeys Newton's first law? Try different angles of launching to test your hypothesis.

- Construct your own version of Galileo's experiment in which a ball is rolled down a slope and up another one. The two slopes should be close to each other. You may use any ball. Keep a record. What can you do to improve the experiment to get the ball to rise upward to the maximum height? How well do your methods work?

- How did Newton build upon Galileo's work to develop the first law? Investigate and discuss.

- The two greatest geniuses of physics are considered by many to be Isaac Newton and Albert Einstein. Compare their lives and works.

Experiment 1.3

Friction

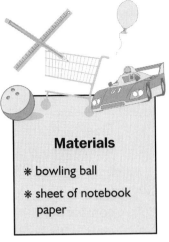

Place a bowling ball or other heavy ball on a sheet of notebook paper. Slowly pull the paper toward you. What happens to the ball?

Materials

* bowling ball
* sheet of notebook paper

You can expect to find that when the paper is pulled slowly, both ball and paper move toward you.

Why does this result differ from Experiment 1.1, where the ball stayed in place when the paper was rapidly pulled away? The explanation may be summed up in one word: *friction*.

Friction is a force that arises whenever two surfaces meet, and it always opposes motion. If an object moves forward, friction will slow it down. If the same object moves backward, friction still slows it down.

In the case of the ball on paper, the friction between the ball and the paper holds the ball to the paper unless a greater force than the friction is exerted. This is what happens if the sheet is quickly pulled from under the ball. When the paper is pulled slowly, the smaller force exerted is not enough to overcome the friction between the sheet and ball. They move together when pulled.

Since friction is always involved in motion on our Earth, it is a topic to which this book will return again and again as motion is examined.

Project Idea and Further Investigation

Compare different surfaces to determine which slows a bowling ball the least, that is, which provides the least amount of friction. For example, try ice, a Formica countertop, asphalt, paper, etc. Also try pieces of the same material that have different degrees of smoothness. How are the results for the same material affected by the smoothness of the surface?

Experiment 1.4

Second Law: Force and Acceleration

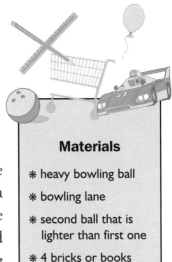

Newton's second law states that the change in speed of an object over a given time is proportional to the force exerted on it. It may be stated mathematically by the following equation:

$$\text{Force} = \text{mass x acceleration, or } F = ma$$

Acceleration is defined as the change in speed of an object divided by the time in which the change takes place.

A bowling ball thrown along an alley will be used to examine Newton's second law of motion. You probably have enough experience with throwing balls to predict that the more force you exert to throw the ball, the faster it will go. This agrees with Newton's second law. As F increases, a also increases (same ball, so the same m). If force decreases, so does the acceleration.

At this point, it is important to recognize that speed and acceleration are not the same thing. Let's look at this by doing an experiment. Be sure to get the permission of the bowling alley manager for this.

Roll the ball down the lane while slapping it onward at intervals with about the same force each time. If you cannot do this at a bowling alley, use an ordinary rubber ball on a smooth floor. What happens?

You will have to chase the ball to keep applying the same force at intervals. The ball should keep going faster and faster.

Has the force that you are applying changed? Hopefully, it has not, yet the ball keeps speeding up. How can this be?

The explanation lies in the variable, acceleration. Acceleration measures the change in velocity that takes place over a certain time.

$$\text{Acceleration} = \frac{\text{final velocity} - \text{starting velocity}}{\text{time}}$$

For example, for an object moving in a straight line, the acceleration might be the change in speed in miles per hour that takes place each second. Suppose that the ball was started by a slap that left it going 1 mile per hour (1 mph). You slap it at the end of one more second to go 2 mph. The acceleration is the difference in speed divided by the time that it takes, so the acceleration is

$$\frac{2 \text{ mph} - 1 \text{ mph}}{1s} = \frac{1 \text{ mph}}{s}$$

Each second that you speed up the ball, you make it go 1 mph faster than before, so that at the end of 5 seconds, for example, the ball is moving at 5 mph. The same force gives the same acceleration each time, but the speed keeps changing. You have to keep chasing after the ball to keep your hand on it because you are speeding it up all the time with the same acceleration.

You probably also have enough experience with balls to know that the heavier the ball is, the harder it is for you to throw it to get the same acceleration. In other words, the same push given to a billiard ball and a bowling ball will cause the much lighter billiard ball to go much farther.

Project Ideas and Further Investigations

* Test Newton's second law in another way. Investigate what happens when mass instead of acceleration is your variable. Plan to carry out the experiment with as little friction as possible. A bowling ball on a plank raised at one end can be used to provide the same force each time. Allow the same ball to impact different bowling balls or other balls of different weights. The descending ball must hit each of the others dead center. Measure the change in speed over time for each ball that is hit. Keep in mind that each ball has zero speed when hit. Once the ball is rolling, you can measure its speed (final speed) by finding how long it takes to cover a measured length of the lane. One or more helpers with stopwatches are needed.

  Were you able to verify the mathematical form of the second law? Explain. Construct a graph of mass versus acceleration and explain the shape of the graph.

* Based on Newton's second law, $F = ma$, explain why a bowler would prefer to throw a heavier ball than a lighter one to knock down the pins. Draw a diagram explaining your hypothesis. Find and list other examples of the relationship involved. You might use a bowling ball descending from different heights on a plank to gather data. Report on the outcomes.

Experiment 1.5

Third Law: Action and Reaction Are Equal

Materials

* strong, smooth wooden plank, at least 120 cm (4 ft) long and 20 cm (8 in) wide

* gutter in bowling lane

* 4 books, each about 2.5 cm (1 in) thick

* meterstick or yardstick

* pencil

* 4 bowling balls, 2 about the same weight, 1 weighing more, and 1 weighing less

According to Newton's third law, every time a force is exerted on an object, the object exerts an equal force right back.

Newton's third law is, perhaps, the most amazing of the three laws. It may be hard to believe, at first, that every time you exert a force on something, it exerts an equal force back on you. Let's look at how bowling balls act when they hit each other.

As before, obtain permission from the supervisor of a bowling alley or other location before carrying out the following experiment.

Place a smooth wooden plank on the alley floor before the foul line and in line with one of the gutters (the troughs on either side). The gutter will help you to roll balls in line with each other. If you carry out the experiment in a location other than a bowling alley, you will need to place barriers on the floor so that the balls will roll along a straight path. Raise the back end of the plank by placing two books under it. You now have a slope down which to roll a bowling ball into the gutter. Mark a line with a pencil about 15 cm (6 in) from the top of the plank.

Select two bowling balls that weigh about the same. Place one ball in the gutter about 60 cm (2 ft) from the foul line. Hold the other ball at the mark you made on the plank. Let the ball roll down the plank and into the gutter, as shown in Figure 4.

What happens to the ball in the gutter? What happens to the descending ball?

Will the same thing happen if the descending ball moves faster? Place two more books under the plank and allow the

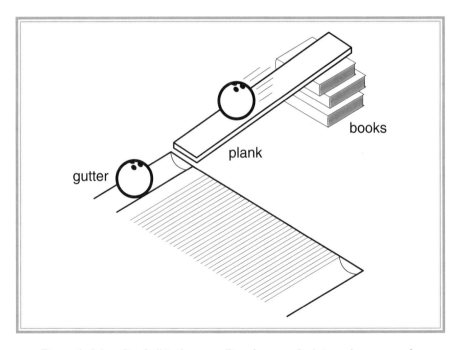

Figure 4. A bowling ball is shown rolling down a plank into the gutter of a bowling lane. Another ball is in the gutter not far from the plank. The arrangement allows the descending ball to hit the stationary ball in the gutter at its center. Balls of different weights can be placed into the gutter. Each time, the descending ball exerts a force on the ball in the gutter. The ball in the gutter exerts an opposite force on the descending one, according to Newton's third law of motion.

ball to roll down the plank to hit the other ball as before. Observe.

In both cases, the descending ball stops when it hits the ball in the gutter. The gutter ball starts moving. When the descending ball goes down faster, the gutter ball moves away faster. This is because the descending ball with the greater acceleration exerts a greater force on the gutter ball.

When the descending ball goes with a higher velocity than before to the point of impact, it goes with a greater acceleration than before. A greater acceleration for the same mass means a greater force. That is why the faster descending ball makes the gutter ball move away faster.

Why does the descending ball stop? Only a force acting upon it could have stopped it. That force could only have come from the ball in the gutter. The force from the ball in the gutter was equal but opposite in direction to the one it experienced.

Did the second ball make it to the pins at the end of the lane? Often, the answer is no. This is because the surface of the gutter is rough. Friction rapidly slows the ball to a halt even though the gutter slants slightly downward.

What do you think will happen if a heavier ball hits a lighter one? What do you predict will happen if a lighter ball hits a heavier one?

Place one of the first two bowling balls into the gutter as before. Hold a heavier ball at the mark on the plank. Release the ball as before. Does the descending ball stop? Does the other ball move?

Remove the heavier ball and set it aside. Place the other bowling ball back in the gutter as before. Set the lightest ball on the mark on the plank. Release it. What happens to both balls? How do you explain the results?

When the heavier ball hits the ball in the gutter, the heavier ball slows down but keeps rolling. At the same time, the ball in the gutter (lighter ball) moves rapidly away. To explain this, consider that the third law says that each ball will exert an equal but opposite force on the other one. The first ball, with its larger mass, m_1, exerts a force, labeled as F, when it hits the gutter ball. The gutter ball has a lesser mass, m_2, so it moves off with a greater acceleration, a_2. At the same time, the gutter ball exerts an equal force, F, back on the descending ball. Since the descending ball has a larger mass, m_1, the force, F, is not enough to stop it. The descending ball is slowed but keeps rolling.

action	reaction
$F = m_1 a_1$	$F = m_2 a_2$
$\mathbf{O}$	$\circ$

$$F \ = \ F$$
$$\text{since } m_1 \ > \ m_2,$$
$$a_1 \ < \ a_2$$

When a lighter ball hits a heavier one, the lighter ball moves backward while the heavier one moves forward. This is similarly explained by the third law. The forces are equal and opposite, so the same sized force pushes the heavier one forward but stops the lighter ball and rolls it backward.

Did you ever turn on the water in a hose lying on the ground with its spray nozzle open? The hose probably started to whip around, spraying everything within reach. This was because the squirting water exerted an equal force back on the hose. You can see why such a tremendous, strong concrete pad is needed under a NASA rocket upon launching.

Does the third law mean that when you lean on a wall, the wall is leaning on you? Certainly. Otherwise, you and the wall would fall down.

The next chapters will provide additional ways to understand Newton's three laws of motion.

Project Idea and Further Investigation

In terms of Newton's third law, show what forces are involved when (1) a bowler picks up a ball, (2) walks (or runs) forward with it, (3) swings it backward, (4) swings it forward, and (5) releases it. Make diagrams to illustrate the equal and opposite forces.

Chapter 2

Newton in the Supermarket

Shoppers who push a cart full of groceries or are trying to rush through the express checkout counter are not likely to be thinking about how the laws of physics affect their motion. Yet their motion and that of the cart is governed by Newton's three laws.

The motion of a cart in a supermarket differs in an important way from the motion of a bowling ball on a bowling lane. It is not that the bowling ball slides smoothly ahead whereas shoppers in a supermarket are meandering about. Rather, it is that a bowling ball travels on a bowling lane with a minimum of friction. At the supermarket, however, friction is a major hindrance to the motion of a cart.

Friction is always present in our world. It is a force that appears wherever two surfaces meet. We can never see friction, but we can observe its effects. Friction between stationary surfaces in contact is called static friction. Friction between surfaces that are sliding over each other (only one moving surface is necessary) is called sliding friction, or kinetic friction.

Much of the material in this chapter will examine how friction affects a moving object and plays a part in Newton's three laws. A great deal can be learned by just observing what happens when different pushes and pulls are exerted on a supermarket cart and what happens to different groceries as they are pushed and pulled.

NOTE: When an experiment in this chapter calls for a super-market shopping cart, be sure that the cart is in excellent condition with wheels that are clean and not worn, bent, or rusty.

Experiment 2.1

First Law and a Shopping Cart: Inertia

Materials

* shopping cart at supermarket

* 7–9-oz rectangular cardboard box from supermarket shelf

* 8-oz round can of food

* adult

Newton's first law states that an object will stay at rest or move without changing velocity unless acted on by a force (see Figures 5a and 5b).

On the supermarket shelves, find an unopened cardboard box that weighs 7 to 9 oz, such as a box of muffin mix. Also, find an 8-oz round can such as a can of tomato sauce. Place both items near each other inside the basket of a supermarket shopping cart at the driver's end. The box should rest on its largest side, while the can should be upright.

Have an adult push the cart forward very rapidly for a few seconds and then stop it very suddenly. Observe what happens to the objects in the cart.

If the can does not move or moves only a bit, the cart was probably not halted all at once. Try it again. The cart might also need to be pushed with more force, especially if it has a plastic basket rather than a metal one. Try to get the can to move at least a third of the length of the basket. What happens to the box? Why? What does all this have to do with Newton's first law? Replace the can and box on the shelves.

At the start, the shopping cart, the can, and the box are all at rest. When the cart is pushed forward, the box and

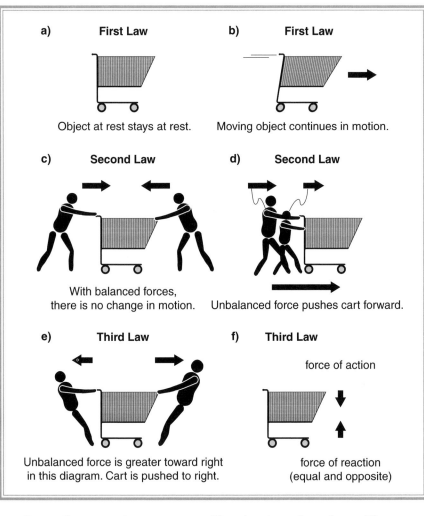

Figure 5. NEWTON'S THREE LAWS. The drawings show how different combinations of pushes and pulls (forces) affect the motion of a supermarket shopping cart, in accordance with Newton's three laws. Each arrow in a drawing shows the direction of a force. The length of the arrow indicates the comparative size of the force.

a. First law: Object at rest stays at rest.

b. First law: Moving object continues its motion.

c. Second law: With balanced forces, there is no change in motion.

d. Second law: Unbalanced force pushes cart forward.

e. Second law: When unbalanced force is greater toward right, cart is pushed to right.

f. Third law: Force of reaction is equal and opposite to force of action.

the can move with it. Static friction holds the box and can to the bottom of the basket. When the cart is suddenly stopped, the box has enough friction holding it to the basket so that it stops suddenly, too. There is much less friction between the can and the basket. As a result, the can keeps moving, as predicted by Newton's first law. It may go halfway forward in the basket before friction stops it.

Did Newton ever have to pour ketchup from the bottom of a glass ketchup bottle? Very unlikely, but if the bottle looked anything like the one in today's supermarket, Newton would have done it very simply. He would have turned the bottle upside down, plunged it downward, and then stopped it very suddenly. Now you can explain how to get ketchup out of a bottle in terms of Newton's first law.

Project Ideas and Further Investigations

- Investigate the conveyer belt at the checkout counter. Why don't the groceries keep moving ahead when the belt stops, as predicted by Newton's first law? What change might cause this to take place? Arrange to try it and explain the results.

- You can use the method of Experiment 2.1 to investigate how the friction of a solid depends upon its surface properties. Find objects that have similar shapes and weights but are made of different materials. For example, a pair of sardine cans, one bare and one boxed, can be compared. Seek out other similar matched objects as well. You could also cover the bottom of an object with different materials such as clear thin plastic wrap, aluminum foil, or shiny wrapping paper. For all, the surface should be taut and unwrinkled. For each test, start and suddenly stop the cart with an object in it at the driver's end. Compare how far each member of the pair of objects slides. Construct a table listing materials in order of surface friction.

Experiment 2.2

Second Law and a Shopping Cart: Balanced and Unbalanced Forces

Materials

* shopping cart
* 2 friends
* long-handled broom

Suppose you are pushing a shopping cart in a supermarket. Along comes a school friend who gets in front of the cart and starts pushing it back at you. You both push equally, laughing aloud at each other. The cart stays in place (Figure 5c). Finally, your friend gives up and comes around to talk to you.

Since you were both pushing, each of you was exerting a force. According to Newton's second law, a force should cause acceleration. But the cart was standing still. However, one force can balance an opposing equal force, causing the two to cancel each other out.

When forces act to cancel each other out, they are said to be balanced. No acceleration results. The object upon which the balanced forces act either keeps moving in the same direction as before or stays at rest as before. Each force would have caused acceleration if not canceled by the other.

What happens when the forces do not cancel each other out, when they are unbalanced? What would occur with each of the following?

You push the cart by yourself. Then you are joined by your friend pushing with you. What happens? See Figure 5d.

You pull the cart backward but your friend pulls back on the cart harder than you do. What happens this time? See Figure 5e.

You push the cart forward harder than your friend pushes it back at you. What happens?

Make a rule for unbalanced forces acting in line with each other.

Here is one way of stating the rule. When forces in line with each other act on the same object, they are added together when going in the same direction. They are subtracted from each other when their directions are opposite. That is, the cart moves faster when you both push together in the same direction. When one of you pushes in one direction and the other pushes in the opposite direction, the cart is always slowed. The direction the cart ends up taking is determined by the stronger push.

Is a force acting on a cart that is standing still with nobody touching it? Earlier in this book, you might have said no, since the cart is not moving. However, the weight of the cart exerts a force due to gravity, and that force acts upon the ground. The ground pushes the cart back up, in accord with Newton's third law. If the ground were soft, it would not be able to exert as much of a push and the cart would sink. When the cart stays in place, downward and upward forces are balanced. See Figure 5f.

When forces operate, both size and direction must be considered. A quantity that must be described by both size and direction is called a vector quantity. Force is a vector because it depends on both size and direction.

Based on experience, what do you think will happen if your friend pushes the handle of the cart at the same time that you do but at an angle toward one side? Where will the cart head? Try it if you are not sure. What is the rule for this?

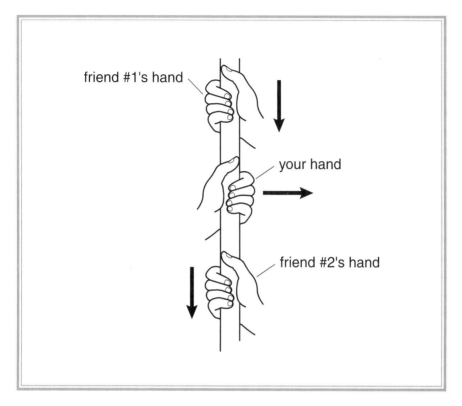

friend #1's hand

your hand

friend #2's hand

Figure 6. Two people push the handle of a broomstick downward while a third person pushes it sideways. Since the stick always moves sideways, more or less, the broomstick cannot be made to go straight down.

When forces are at an angle to each other, they will push the object to one side, the angle depending on which force is stronger.

Ask two friends to hold a broom handle vertically directly above a target spot on the floor. Each should hold it on the same side by one hand. You hold the handle between their two hands and push sideways toward them (see Figure 6). Tell them to push the broom handle straight down, directly toward the target. They must not push it at an angle. Can they get it to touch the target? Why?

Your friends can never push the broom onto the target. The sideways push always prevents the broom from going straight down.

Project Ideas and Further Investigations

- When two or more forces act upon the same object, the size and direction of the force that results can be determined by a simple process called vector analysis. Look up this process in any physics book. Plan and execute a series of forces in different directions on an object such as a shopping cart or a small toy car. You can use approximate forces on the object unless you are planning an investigation that will include measurements of acceleration, too. Predict the approximate direction of the object at the end, based upon vector analysis. How well does the prediction correspond to the actual results? Explain.

  - Use vector analysis to show why the broomstick in Experiment 2.2 can never be pushed down on the target by the two friends.

Experiment 2.3

Static Friction

Whenever the surfaces of two solids are in contact, there are attractive forces between them. These attractive forces are electrostatic, coming from within the atoms and molecules that make up the solids. The result of the attractions is that the solids resist being pulled apart. Force is needed to slide one solid away from the other. The resistance to the separation of stationary surfaces is called static friction.

You can observe static friction in the following activity. Whenever you carry out any of the remaining experiments in this chapter in a supermarket, **ask permission of the supermarket manager.** Read the instructions in advance so that you and the adult helping you can assure the manager that there will be no damage or interference and that everything will be returned to its place. If you have the needed groceries and a smooth vinyl or a wooden floor at home, you may carry out Experiment 2.3 and some of the later experiments at home.

Obtain from the shelves a large, sealed plastic or metal cylindrical container. The contents must not shift when tilted. The heavier the sealed container, the better. A large plastic jar

Materials

* large, sealed plastic or metal cylindrical container filled with contents that do not move when tilted, such as a jar of peanut butter or a can of concentrated creamy soup

* smooth, level floor

* sewing elastic, 0.6 cm (¼ in) wide and at least 75 cm (30 in) long, usually found in packets on racks in the sewing section of stores

* a partner

* measuring tape

of peanut butter or a can of thick soup such as concentrated mushroom or split pea soup will do. Place the cylindrical container upright on a smooth, level vinyl or wood floor in an empty aisle.

Obtain a strip of sewing elastic that is 0.6 cm (¼ in) wide and at least 75 cm (30 in) long. Tie one end of the elastic tape around the middle of the upright container with a firm knot. Hold the tape fully extended without stretching and measure the length of the tape from the knot to the free end.

Gently pull the tape horizontally by the free end, gradually increasing the pull until the container just begins to move. Repeat while your partner measures the length of the elastic just before the jar moves. See Figure 7.

The cylindrical container and the elastic will be used again in the next experiment.

When this experiment was carried out using an upright cylindrical 40-oz plastic jar of peanut butter on a vinyl floor, an 81-cm (32-in) length of elastic was stretched to 153 cm (60 in) to overcome static friction. How do your results compare?

Static friction arises from molecular attractions, not from the weight of the container. Weight can affect the size of the friction (as you will see later), but it does not cause it.

Static friction depends not only on the materials that make up the solids but also on such variables as humidity, finish of the surface, and cleanliness of the surface. Films of air, oxides, or lubricants between the surfaces all act to reduce static friction. However, if the surfaces are totally clean and are placed together in a vacuum, static friction

Figure 7. A strip of sewing elastic is tied to an upright jar. The length of the elastic is measured from the jar to the free end. Then the jar is pulled by the elastic until it moves. The difference in length between the stretched and unstretched elastic is an indication of the strength of the static friction between the jar and the surface it stands on.

may become so strong that the surfaces cleave together. Space and moon explorations have to take this into account to make sure that certain instruments do not stop operating. (To see whether surface area plays a role in friction, see Experiment 2.6.)

Project Ideas and Further Investigations

Investigate static friction of various solids. The length of a strip of sewing elastic as used in Experiment 2.3 or a spring fishing scale may be used to compare frictional forces. Each sample should have about the same weight. Weights can be adjusted by placing objects on top of the solid. All tests should be made using the same flooring. Try cardboard, plastic jugs, metal cans, objects smoothly wrapped in foil, paper, vinyl tiles, wood, felt, carpeting, and so on. Do not use surfaces such as sandpaper that could damage the floor. Which materials tend to produce the greatest static friction? Arrange the materials in order of their tendency to produce static friction.

Experiment 2.4

Sliding and Rolling Friction

We all know from experience that a supermarket cart slows down and stops unless you keep pushing it. But Newton's first law says that a cart should keep going at the same speed without any help once you get it going. In fact, according to the second law, if you keep exerting a force on the cart, the cart should keep speeding up. Are Newton's laws being contradicted?

No, Newton's laws are not being contradicted. Friction exerts an opposing force that slows the cart. The same attractive forces that cause static friction also cause sliding friction when one surface moves over another. To keep a cart moving at a steady speed, you have to push it just hard enough to overcome the opposing friction. The cart then keeps moving onward at the same speed in agreement with the first law of motion. Should you want to speed up the cart, you would need to apply an additional force.

Sliding friction, also called kinetic friction, takes place whenever one surface slides over another one. A box pushed along a floor and a bowling ball moving along a bowling lane develop sliding friction. You have probably encountered sliding friction when you were pushing a stubborn shopping cart and discovered that one wheel was stuck at an angle to the direction you were trying to go. When that happened, the cart was sliding instead of rolling.

When a supermarket cart rolls along, some of the friction comes from the contact between the wheels and the floor. Rolling friction, however, is usually quite small. The greater part of the friction on a rolling cart most probably comes from the bushings (bearings) of the wheels. As you move the cart, the wheels turn around the stationary axle. The bushings between the wheel and the axle, usually ball bearings, reduce the friction of the wheel and enable it to turn. The difference between the magnitudes of rolling and sliding friction can be observed by rolling and sliding a cylindrical object.

Use the same cylindrical container as in Experiment 2.3. Place this container on its side in an open space or empty aisle on a smooth, level, wooden or vinyl floor. Give the container a slight push. Watch it roll. How far does it go?

Place the same container upright. Give it about the same push that you gave it when on its side. How far does it move?

Repeat this with a different cylindrical container.

Given only a slight push, the rolling containers move 1.5 to 3 m (5 to 10 feet) or more along a level floor. The upright containers probably do not move at all. Sliding friction is much greater than rolling friction.

How much force is needed to get one of the containers to slide when upright? Also, which is bigger, static friction or sliding friction? To make comparisons, you will need a measuring tape, sewing elastic 0.6 cm (¼ in) wide and at least 75 cm (30 in) long, and a partner to help.

Tie one end of the elastic firmly around the middle of the same upright container that you used in Experiment 2.3. With the aid of your partner, measure the length of the elastic strip held straight out, without stretching, from the knot to the free end of the strip.

Pull the free end of the elastic strip, holding the strip horizontally, until the container is slowly moving. Keep pulling it so that it slides at a slow and steady pace. With the aid of your partner, measure the length of the stretched elastic. When you release stretched elastic, the elastic may snap painfully against your helper's fingers, so return the elastic to its unstretched length before letting go of it. Return all groceries to the shelves.

To get a 1 kg (40-oz) jar of peanut butter to slide on a vinyl floor, our data showed that the elastic stretched from 81 cm (32 in) to 140 cm (55 in). The measured sliding friction was slightly less than the static friction measured for the same container in Experiment 2.3. The data that you obtain will depend upon the material of the container, its weight, the elastic, and the flooring that you use.

Sliding friction can also result from other forces besides intermolecular attractions between surfaces. If one surface is harder than the other, the harder surface may plow into the softer one, deforming it and increasing the friction. As with static friction, sliding friction may be decreased by films of dirt, oxides, or lubricants on the surfaces.

Project Ideas and Further Investigations

- Use the same sliding object on different surfaces to compare sliding frictions. The size of the friction may be measured with sewing elastic as in Experiment 2.4, or you can measure how far a torsion spring or a fisherman's scale, available in hardware stores, is stretched. Test surfaces such as wood, vinyl, smooth aluminum foil, cement, asphalt, polyurethane foam, sandpaper, different types of carpeting, etc. You may even be lucky enough to find a safe patch of ice to try (in the right location at the right time of year). **Never experiment near a frozen lake or pond without adult supervision**. Arrange the surfaces in a list in order of the friction they produce.

- How is rolling friction affected by different surfaces? Does the material make a difference? Does the smoothness make a difference? Does the hardness make a difference? To find out, measure how far the rolling object moves on each surface given the same push each time. The same force can be exerted each time on the object to start it rolling by letting it roll down a board that is slightly elevated at one end.

- How do ball bearings work to reduce friction? Investigate different ways that ball bearings are used, and write a paper on the topic.

- You can get an idea of the amount of bearing friction in the wheels of a supermarket cart by attaching a length of elastic to the handle of a cart and comparing the stretched length for a rolling cart to the unstretched length. It may be necessary to use an elastic tape that can withstand a greater stretching force than was used in Experiment 2.4, such as one with a width of 2.5 cm (1 in). Assume that most of the friction is due to the bearings. Try several carts in the same store, preferably including one with a plastic basket and one with a metal basket, and then try those in another store. Discuss and explain the results.

Experiment 2.5

Sliding Friction and Weight

Does sliding friction increase as an object is made heavier? To find out, take a cylindrical can such as a coffee can from the supermarket or pantry shelf. Place the can upright on a smooth floor.

Tie a strip of elastic 0.6 cm (¼ in) wide and about 100 cm (39 in) long around the middle of the upright can. Pull the free end of the elastic to observe how the elastic stretches while the can is sliding.

Materials

* can of coffee or other large cylindrical can

* smooth floor

* sewing elastic, 0.6 cm (¼ in) wide and about 100 cm (39 in) long

* 2–3 bricks of ground coffee (rectangular packages tightly packed in heavy foil) or other weights

Obtain a coffee brick (or other weight) and place it on top of the can. Again pull the free end of the elastic and observe how the elastic stretch compares this time.

Place another coffee brick on top of the first one and repeat pulling the assembly. If you need to be sure about your conclusion, you may want to try a third brick. Return the groceries to where they belong on the shelves.

You can expect to find that the greater the weight being pulled on the same base, the longer is the length of the elastic. Correspondingly, the greater is the sliding friction. It was Leonardo da Vinci (1452–1519) who first noted that friction increases with load.

To understand why friction increases as weight increases, imagine that you are looking at a smooth surface such as the rim of a metal can. When you use a strong magnifying glass to look at the rim, you discover that the surface is not really even. An even stronger magnifier shows tiny irregularities and undulations. This unevenness means that the rim does not fully contact the surface beneath it. Only the higher points are touching. Weight acts as a force to press the surfaces closer together. More of the surface area makes real contact. Hence, friction increases with weight.

Project Ideas and Further Investigations

- Investigate the relationship between weight and static friction.
- For sliding friction and for static friction, does the friction increase proportionately with weight? That is, when the weight doubles or triples, does the friction double or triple correspondingly?
- Recently, the nature of material surfaces has received much investigation. Scanning microscopes and other instruments have obtained photographs of surfaces at the molecular level. Locate some of these photographs in scientific publications or on the Internet (you may have to contact a researcher on this topic to help you). Examine these photographs to find examples of unevenness in the surface that may lead to friction. What can you find out about the friction produced by the materials that were investigated?
- Why is rolling friction so much less than sliding friction? Write a report on the current thinking about it. Hypothesize your own explanation. Perhaps you can invent a test for your hypothesis.

Experiment 2.6

Sliding Friction and Surface Area

Materials

* large rectangular box of detergent or wooden block

* smooth floor

* string long enough to tie around the largest part of the box

* tape measure

* sewing elastic about 0.6 cm (¼ inch) wide and about 90–120 cm (3–4 ft) long

* a partner

Does sliding friction increase as the area between the surfaces increases?

This can be investigated with the aid of a box whose length, width, and height are each different. The surfaces should all be of similar smoothness. A large box of detergent may be used, or you may choose to use a wooden block.

Place the box on a smooth floor. Turn it to rest on the surface with the largest area. Obtain a piece of string long enough to go all the way around the box horizontally and a length of sewing elastic that is about 0.6 cm (¼ in) wide and about 90–120 cm (3–4 ft) long. Tie the string around the box, then tie one end of the elastic to the string. With the aid of your partner, measure the extended, unstretched length of elastic from the knot to the free end. Slowly pull the free end of the elastic horizontally to keep the box sliding at a steady pace. The length is an indication of the strength of the sliding friction. (See Figure 8.) What are the lengths of the elastic before and while pulling the box?

Turn the box onto a different side; reset the string and elastic. Knot the elastic so that the unstretched length is the same as before. Again, pull the box along horizontally. Measure the length of the stretched elastic while pulling the box.

Turn the box so that it rests on the third side. Reset the string and elastic as before, pull the box along, and note the length of the elastic. Return the box to the shelf.

Which is greater, the force needed to pull the box along when it is on its biggest side or its smallest side? Suggest an explanation for your observations.

You can expect to find that the area between the surfaces doesn't make any difference. Friction does not depend on area of contact. Again, it was Leonardo da Vinci who first stated this. His discoveries about friction were, unfortunately, neglected for many years.

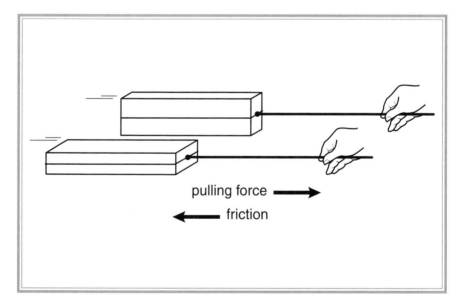

Figure 8. The sliding friction of a box is measured on each of its three different sides by pulling the box with a sewing elastic. The lengths the elastic stretches are compared for each side to see which area shows the greatest sliding friction. The drawing shows the lengths of the stretched elastic tapes for two of the sides.

The accepted explanation for the independence of friction from area has to do with effective area in contact. An increase in weight on a specific area pushes the uneven surfaces closer so as to increase the area actually in contact (the effective area). If the area over which the weight acts is increased, the weight is spread out more and there is lessened contact. The result is that the effective area remains the same. The friction remains the same.

Experiments 2.5 and 2.6 have shown that sliding friction increases with weight but is independent of the area of contact.

Project Idea and Further Investigation

Are the results of Experiment 2.6 applicable to all materials no matter how hard or how soft? Test the relationship between weight and contact area on materials of different hardnesses.

Experiment 2.7

Third Law: Equal and Opposite Paired Forces

<table>
<tr><td colspan="1">Materials</td></tr>
<tr><td>

* skateboard, in-line skates, or low wagon

* helmet

* heavy ball

* shopping cart

* strong cord at least 120 cm (4 ft) long

</td></tr>
</table>

Newton's third law can be illustrated with a shopping cart and another object with wheels on which you stand. The object with wheels may be a skateboard, in-line skates, or a low wagon in which you can sit. In any case, the wheels should be able to move freely and the ground should be smooth as with a wooden gym floor or a vinyl tile floor. If you use the low wagon or in-line skates, modify the following instructions accordingly.

Wearing a helmet, stand firmly with both feet on a skateboard holding a heavy ball such as a medicine ball. Toss the ball into a shopping cart about 60 cm (2 ft) in front of you. What happens to you and your skateboard? See Figure 9a.

Stand on the skateboard and start to throw the ball as before, but this time don't let go of it. What happens this time? Put the ball away.

Place your skateboard with one end against a wall. Without standing on it, push the skateboard toward the wall. See Figure 9b. Does the skateboard move? Does the wall move?

Stand on the skateboard while it has one end touching the wall. Slowly, push with your hands against the wall. See Figure 9c. What happens this time?

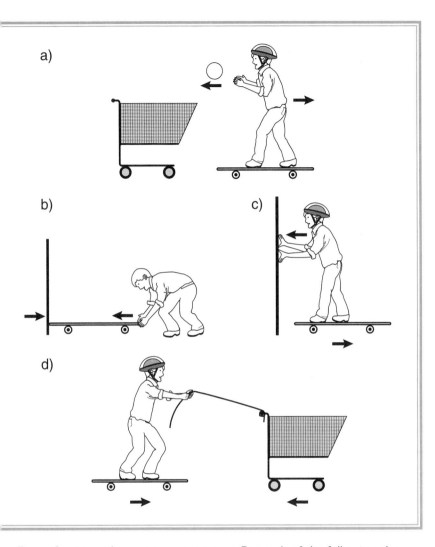

Figure 9. NEWTON'S THIRD LAW ON WHEELS. For each of the following, the forces are equal in size and opposite in direction:

a) A heavy ball is tossed toward a nearby shopping cart by a person standing on a skateboard. The arrows show the direction that the ball goes and the direction that the skateboard moves after the toss.

b) A skateboard is pushed against a wall. No motion takes place.

c) A person pushes against a wall while standing on a skateboard. The arrows show the direction of the push and the direction that the skateboard moves.

d) A person on a skateboard pulls a supermarket cart closer with a cord. The arrows show the direction that each moves.

Tie a cord at least 120 cm (4 ft) long to the handle of a shopping cart. Hold the other end of the cord as you stand on a skateboard several feet behind the cart. Pull the cart toward you. What happens to the cart? What happens to you? See Figure 9d.

How do you explain each of the above? Each illustrates Newton's third law.

The following describes what most likely happened.

When you tossed the ball forward while standing on the skateboard, the skateboard moved backward. You exerted a force on the ball to push it forward. According to the third law, the ball exerted an equal and opposite force on you, pushing you back on your skateboard.

When you stood on the cart and started to throw the ball but didn't let go of it, you and the ball both ended up as before. No unbalanced force acted on the ball, and therefore no opposite force acted on you.

Then you exerted a force on the skateboard by pushing it against a wall. Nothing appeared to happen. The skateboard stayed where it was, and so did the wall. What happened to the force you exerted? Since there was no change, the force you exerted must have been balanced by another force. According to Newton, the wall had to be pushing back on the skateboard.

Next, you stood on the skateboard while you pushed the wall. The wall pushed back at you. Since the skateboard was free to move, you and the skateboard moved away from the wall.

Finally, you pulled a shopping cart toward you while you were standing on a skateboard. The cart moved toward you and you moved toward the cart. You pulled the cart, so the cart pulled you.

All of the above are examples of the paired forces of Newton's third law. For each, the forces are equal but opposite in direction

Every force involves Newton's third law.

Project Ideas and Further Investigations

- How does the spring scale used in the produce department of the supermarket illustrate Newton's third law? What are the paired forces? How are they equalized? What happens to the scale before the forces equalize? Find other examples in a supermarket of how Newton's third law operates and explain them. Use diagrams as needed. Among others, consider how a shopper can walk, how a package can be taken down from a shelf, what happens to the hose that squirts water to clean the shelves, and so on. Compile your information in a report about how Newton's third law works in a supermarket.

- How does a cyclist apply Newton's third law? For example, how is the pedal moved, how does the wheel act against the ground, and how do the brakes operate? Make diagrams to explain your answers.

Chapter 3

Newton at the Indy 500

"Ladies and gentlemen, start your engines." With these famous words, the Indy 500 race starts. The race is held annually in Indianapolis, Indiana, and is watched on site by more people (over 350,000) than is any other one-day sporting event in the world. Traditionally, it takes place on the Sunday afternoon of the Memorial Day weekend on an oval that is 2½ miles (4 km) long. The *500* stands for the number of miles each car must finish (805 km), a total of 200 laps. Indy cars can go as fast as 240 miles per hour (386 kilometers per hour), which means that they can zip across an entire football field in about one second. Thirty-three cars enter the race after qualifying in a field that may begin with ninety cars. All thirty-three drivers win a prize, depending on where the driver places in the finish. In 2001, the winning driver, Helio Castroneves took home $1.27 million.

Each Indy car has an open cockpit and no fenders over the wheels. The V-8 or V-6 turbocharged engine is behind the driver. Wings, or airfoils, in the front and back hold the car to the ground, as will be examined later in this chapter. The powerful engines in the cars may be leased from a manufacturer, usually with restrictions that prevent the motors from being altered. For cars with those engines, designers must work on the rest of the car to improve its performance.

The first Indianapolis 500 was run on May 30, 1911, on a speedway paved with 3.2 million bricks. Those bricks are still there, covered with asphalt, except for the "yard of bricks," a 36-in (91-cm) strip that remains uncovered at the starting line.

The two major considerations in car racing are speed and safety. How do these rely on Newton's three laws?

Experiment 3.1

Newton and Braking

Materials

* board or strong cardboard
* toy car
* 4–5 books
* pencil
* tape
* Ping-Pong ball
* golf ball
* ball of oil-based clay

The brake is one of the most important and necessary parts of a racing car. What happens to the driver when a car is suddenly braked? A toy car will be used to simulate the car on the road, and objects placed on the car can simulate different riders. The car will be set into motion by allowing it to roll down a hill.

Obtain a board or length of strong cardboard. Raise one end by piling two to three books under it. A barrier will be needed at the lower end of the board to stop or slow the car. Tape a pencil across the width of the plank near the lower end to serve as the barrier.

Any toy car at least 7 cm (at least 2¾ in) long may be used. A Ping-Pong ball will act as the rider. The rider can be set anywhere on the car as long as it stays in place until the car hits the barrier (see Figure 10).

Set the car with its rider near the high end of the board. What do you think will happen to the rider after the car rolls down the board and hits the barrier? Will the ball stop, stay on the car, fall off, or go straight ahead? Allow the car to roll down the board. Observe what happens to the car and rider.

How will the results change if the car speeds up? Repeat the experiment, but this time raise the end of the board by adding two more books.

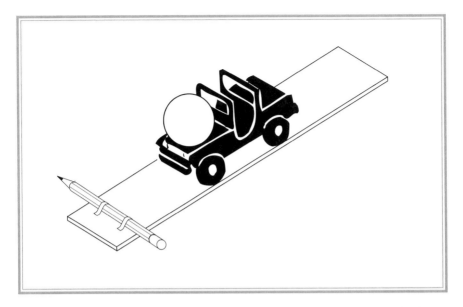

Figure 10. A toy car with a Ping-Pong ball sitting on it rolls down a plank toward a barrier. When it reaches the barrier, the car is stopped. What happens to the ball?

What will happen if a heavier rider is used? Replace the Ping-Pong ball with a golf ball. Allow the car to roll down, as before, at two different speeds (from two different heights). Does the difference in weight affect what happens?

Finally, make a ball of clay and press it onto the car. The ball of clay represents a rider with strong static friction holding it to the car. Predict what will happen when the car and clay rider roll down the board and hit the barrier. What do you observe?

All three riders move with the car as it starts rolling down the board. Car and rider continue to move down the slope together at the same speed and in the same direction. This illustrates Newton's first law—a moving object continues to move at the same speed and in the same direction unless a force acts upon it.

The barrier (pencil) acts as a force to brake the car. The car slows or stops when it hits the barrier, but the Ping-Pong ball and golf ball do not. Both balls continue to move after the car hits the barrier, in accord with Newton's first law. At low car speeds, the Ping-Pong and golf balls may fall a little ahead and to one side, since they are moving slowly. At higher speeds, the balls continue to move ahead, rolling onward once they hit the ground.

The clay ball will probably stick to the car because of its high static friction. It stops when the car stops.

Project Ideas and Further Investigations

- Extend Experiment 3.1 by investigating the following:

    What is the effect of changing the shape of the rider?

    What is the effect of changing the height of the barrier?

    What happens when the toy cars are changed in size, in weight, or in wheel friction?

    What rules can you make about what you observe? Explain your observations in terms of Newton's laws.

- Using the method of Experiment 3.1, gather data and make a chart of the speed of the car versus the forward distance that a ball travels after impact. Graph the data and interpret the graph. What is the importance of this information for drivers?

Experiment 3.2

Rear-End Impact

In a rear-end collision, the force acting on a car pushes it forward, the opposite direction to that of a braking force. What happens to a rider when a car is rear-ended?

Place a toy car on a smooth, hard floor. Set a Ping-Pong ball on the car to act as a rider. With a ruler, sharply whack the back end of the car. What happens to the car? What happens to the rider?

Repeat with a large marble as the rider and observe. Explain your results in terms of Newton's first law.

The car moves forward in response to the whack. The Ping-Pong ball drops downward. The marble does the same thing. Why do the balls drop down instead of moving forward with the car? Newton's first law tells us why: When the car moves forward, there is not enough friction to hold the ball or marble to it. Only the car responds to the whack. Without the car under them to hold them up, gravity pulls the ball and marble straight down.

Similarly, suppose you are sitting in a car that is stopped at a red light. Without warning, you feel the car jerk forward as it is bumped by a car in back of you. What happens to you?

With a rear-end impact, the car moves forward. Your upper body, however, will stay where it was. As a result, your upper body will feel as if it were being pressed into the back of the seat. Actually, your body is hit by the back of the seat. Your shoulders are pushed forward by the seat; your head, since it stays where it was, is snapped back. The result is whiplash—unless you have a headrest to save you.

Indy cars can go from 0 to 100 miles per hour in less than 3 seconds. As far as the driver is concerned, that is like being rear-ended. Indy drivers wear safety helmets, seat belts, fireproof hoods underneath their helmets, and a jumpsuit, shoes, and gloves that are fireproof. Other safety measures are examined in the next experiment.

Experiment 3.3

Safety

How can the rider in a car be protected from a forceful impact or sudden stop?

Materials

* oil-based modeling clay
* toy car
* board
* several books
* steel-edged ruler
* several small strips of wood about the length of the ruler
* 1–2 C-clamps
* short strip of narrow rubber tubing
* scissors
* tape

Shape a piece of clay into a bar that is at least 2.5 cm (1 in) long and about half as wide. The clay bar will represent a passenger in a car. Press it firmly upright on the hood or top of a toy car.

Set up a long board with one end on a pile of several books. A barrier will be needed to act like a dashboard in a real car. To build a barrier, obtain a steel-edged ruler and several strips of wood. Near the lower end of the plank, stack the strips of wood on top of each other across the width of the plank. Place the ruler on top of them so that the steel edge protrudes toward the high end of the board. Use C-clamps to hold the ruler and wood strips tightly to the board.

The steel edge of the ruler represents an unpadded dashboard. When the car is placed on the plank near the ruler, the ruler should be at about the height of the middle of the clay passenger. Check the height of the ruler. Reset the ruler if needed.

Place the car with its passenger at the upper end of the plank. Let it roll downward. What happens to the clay passenger when it hits the "dashboard"?

Slit a short strip of rubber tubing down its length. Pad the steel edge of the ruler by slipping the tubing over it. Tape the tubing in place. Again, release the car with the rider.

What happens to the passenger this time? Use Newton's second law to explain the difference that the padding makes.

Without the padding, the clay passenger receives a deep cut from the steel-edged dashboard. The padding provides better protection. It spreads the force over a larger area instead of concentrating it on the edge. Also, the rubber tubing gives a little as the rider hits it. As a result, it makes the time of impact on the rider a little longer than without padding. If the total time of impact is increased, the acceleration is decreased.

$$\text{Acceleration} = \frac{\text{final velocity} - \text{initial velocity}}{\text{time}}$$

Since $F = ma$ (second law), when the acceleration is smaller, the force of impact is smaller. As a result, the dashboard does less damage. This is why padding is so important.

The bumper on a car acts similarly to increase the time that it takes to bring the car to a halt or to get it moving if rear-ended.

Project Ideas and Further Investigations

- Construct a test car to use for safety measurements. Start with a metal toy car where the chassis and wheelbase are made from separate pieces. Separate the chassis from the base. Attach a sturdy open box firmly onto the wheel base so that the front end of the box slightly overhangs the base. Make a clay figure to act as a seated rider in the car. It can be a torso with no head and no legs below the knees. Place the rider inside at the back of the box. One way to simulate a dashboard is to firmly tape a right-angle metal piece at the model's shoulder height onto the inside front of the box so that one edge points toward the rider. Use this car and dummy to test various safety devices. What kind of padding is most effective on a dashboard? On a bumper?

What kind of seat belt is best to hold the rider in place? Should it be wide or narrow? Should it have give (flexibility)?

What kind of shoulder belt gives the best protection?

How well does an inflated balloon (simulating an air bag) protect the rider?

Does the speed of the car make a difference as to how effective each type of restraint is?

Can you invent another device to protect the rider? If so, describe your idea. If possible, test it and report on the results.

- Use the test car above to examine what happens to a clay figure of a head and torso when a car is impacted from behind. Try out headrests of different shapes, softness, and elasticity. Compare what happens at different speeds.

- All cars at the Indy 500 have padding and harnesses to protect the driver in an accident. Detail all the safety precautions that are taken and explain when and how each one provides protection. Examine helmet protection, too.

Experiment 3.4

Racing Speeds and Friction

Materials

* car or bicycle wheel with tire
* bathroom scale
* concrete or asphalt floor
* smooth wood, vinyl, or linoleum floor
* heavy objects to use to weight the wheel
* rope

An Indy car travels about 75 miles (120 km) between pit stops. Each time the car pulls into the pit, all four tires, worn down by friction, need to be replaced (compared to 60,000 miles for normal tire wear) and the fuel tank has to be refilled—all in less than 17 seconds. The time needed for the pit stops may determine the final winner. Each team is allocated 60 tires for the entire race.

Would you believe that friction is absolutely necessary for the car to move forward? Many of us are accustomed to thinking of friction as a problem because it causes motors to lose energy in the form of heat, which can be damaging. Friction may be undesirable in motors, but not between the car tires and the road.

Newton's third law says that every action causes a simultaneous reaction. In order for a car to move forward, the tires must push backward against the ground. The ground pushes the car forward. It is friction that makes it possible for the tires to grip the ground and push against it. Without friction, the wheels of a car would just spin in place. Tires need traction (that is, friction) to move forward. When a car skids on snow or ice, it is because the tires cannot get a grip on the ground.

Once a race car has started to move at the desired speed, it should continue to move at the same speed and in the same direction, as per the first law. However, that never happens. The engine has to keep going to keep the car moving. Let's see why.

Initially, the engine is needed to overcome the static friction of the car. Then it is needed to increase speed to the desired rate. Once the car is up to speed, the engine must work to balance the forces of rolling friction and internal mechanical friction. Air resistance develops as the car pushes through the air molecules; these molecules are a major source of friction at high speeds. Force is also needed to change the direction of the car as it goes around a curve. Furthermore, the driver may need to slow the car going around a turn but then speed it up again on the straightaway.

Can the wheels go too fast? Yes, they can. If the engine speeds up the wheels too much, the ground cannot generate enough friction to grip the wheels. The force that the tires exert on the ground becomes greater than the frictional force. The car starts to slide instead of roll. A driver cannot control a sliding car; the car cannot be turned, speeded up, or braked. It just continues to go in the same direction at the same speed until something stops it.

To get an idea of the maximum friction to which a tire can respond before it starts to slide (skid), obtain a wheel with a tire on it. If there is none in your garage, perhaps a local auto repair shop will lend you one. You could instead use a bicycle tire on a rim, although the difference in weight will not give you as good an idea of the quantities involved.

When you push the wheel assembly sideways, the force that you must exert to keep it sliding equals the maximum friction. Racing experts call this the adhesive limit of the tire.

To measure the maximum friction, bring the wheel assembly and a bathroom scale to a concrete or asphalt surface. Place the wheel upright on the concrete or asphalt. Push the side of the tire with the flat of your hand low on the wheel until the wheel slides sideways (Figure 11a). Measure how hard you have to push the wheel to just move it along (Figure 11b). To get this measurement, set the bathroom scale between your hand and the tire as you push. The scale should not touch the ground, and you should be able to see the dial. What was the force you exerted to overcome the force of friction?

The force that you exerted equals the maximum friction before the tire starts to slide (skid) on the concrete or asphalt.

Repeat the measurement with the bathroom scale but do it on a smooth wood, vinyl, or linoleum floor. Be sure to obtain permission first from the owner of the floor, and be careful not to damage the floor.

Where was the resistance to sliding greater, on the cement or on the smooth wooden floor? What does this mean with respect to the maximum speed that the car can go on each before it starts to skid?

You will find that the resistance on cement (or on asphalt), measured by this method, is greater than on smooth wood or linoleum by, perhaps, 1½ times. This means that a car will not be able to go as fast on a smooth wooden racetrack before it starts to slide out of control as on a cement one. A sliding (skidding) car cannot be turned, speeded up, or braked. A car

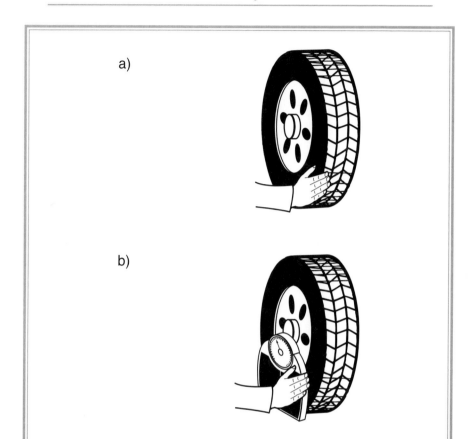

Figure 11. MAXIMUM FRICTION FOR A TIRE (ADHESIVE LIMIT OF THE TIRE)
a. Push with one hand on a wheel to feel the force needed to overcome friction as the wheel slides.
b. Use a bathroom scale to measure the maximum (sliding) friction of the tire.

can exert force against the ground only as long as the tires grip the road.

What do you think will happen to the maximum friction if the tire is heavier? Repeat the experiment on a cement or asphalt surface, but this time add weight to the tire. You can tie some weights onto the wheel with rope. Dumbbells are excellent to use as weights because they can be inserted through the center of the wheel. How does the weight of a car affect the maximum friction? What does that mean with respect to getting a car to go faster?

Recall from Chapter 2 that friction increases with weight. Therefore, the sliding resistance of the tire can be expected to increase with weight. This means that a heavier car can safely go faster than a lighter one on the same road, since it can develop more friction before sliding. However, a heavier car will need a more powerful engine, and the car will use more fuel at the higher speed. As a result, it will have to stop more often to refuel. A race car designer must take all these factors into consideration.

Project Ideas and Further Investigations

- Take a series of measurements using the method of Experiment 3.4 to determine how the weight of a wheel affects sliding friction. Add weights and measure friction until you can no longer overcome the friction with the strength of your arm. Perhaps you can then use a device to provide additional force. Make up a table showing the weight of the wheel and the sliding friction. Graph the results. What trends do you see? Discuss the implications of your results for a racing car.
- Experiment 2.6 suggested that sliding friction is independent of the area of the surfaces in contact. In Experiment 3.4, the maximum sliding friction of an upright tire was measured. Using the

same bathroom scale, measure the sliding friction of the same tire laid on its side. Does this measurement support the conclusion reached in Experiment 2.6? Discuss your results.

- How does the pressure in a tire affect rolling friction? How does it affect sliding friction? Conduct experiments to find out and develop a table of data for comparisons. Develop a hypothesis to explain the results.

- How does the softness of a tire affect rolling friction? A soft tire is one that spreads out more under an applied force than does the same thickness of a hard tire. Before conducting your own experiments, inquire about the matter from manufacturers of tires. Then carry out your own investigations. Be sure to maintain the same pressure in the tires.

- Tires used in drag races are very wide. If contact area does not affect sliding friction, why are the tires so wide? Look for answers on the Internet, and then investigate for yourself.

- Carry out Experiment 3.4 on a surface of linoleum or wood that is covered by a layer of any household or lubricating oil. What happens to the sliding friction? What are the implications for a racing car? Explain. **Under adult supervision**, try the experiment on ice, too.

- How do the treads on a tire affect sliding friction? Search the Internet and library for information on this and write to tire manufacturers for information about their products. Then conduct your own investigation. Also, compare worn treads with new treads. Find out what determines how often the Indy 500 cars have to stop to change tires.

- What is the effect of temperature on rolling and on sliding friction? To find out, select a day when there is a big difference in temperature inside and outside the house or garage.

Experiment 3.5

Getting Around a Curve

Materials

* marble
* golf ball
* ruler with groove down the middle
* scissors
* heavy paper plate with wide rim
* smooth floor
* 2 small weights

When you are in a car that goes rapidly around a sharp left turn, you feel pressed to the right. Why?

Obtain a small marble, a golf ball, and a ruler with a groove down its length.

Cut a heavy paper plate with a wide rim into two sections and arrange them on a smooth surface as shown in Figure 12a. Place a small, heavy weight such as a rock on the cut side of each half to hold it in place. Hold the ruler so that it forms a low ramp down which you can roll a ball to head around the inner side of the plate rim.

Release the marble so that it rolls off the ruler. Does it roll around the inside of the rim? If not, adjust the tilt of the ruler as needed. What happens after the ball rolls around the inside rim? Does it continue to go in a circle?

Repeat with the golf ball, first adjusting the tilt so that you can get it to roll around the rim. Where does it go after that? Explain in terms of Newton's first law.

You will find that each ball rolls around the first half-plate, goes off in a straight line to the other half, rolls around it, and then rolls away in a straight line (see Figure 12b). Newton's first law says that a ball will travel in a straight line unless an external force acts upon it. The ball keeps trying to move in a

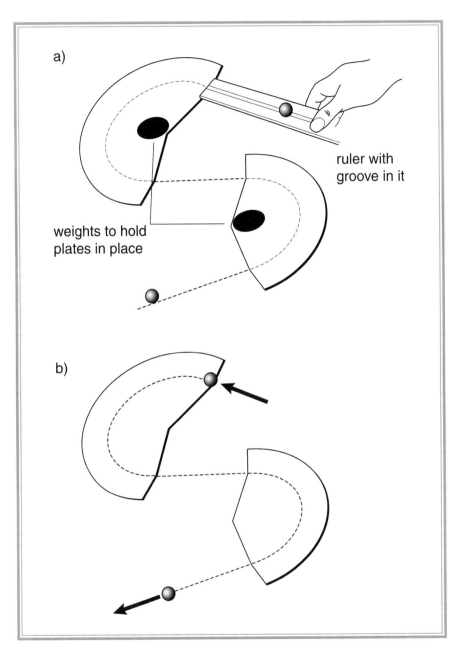

Figure 12. CIRCULAR MOTION

a   A paper plate is cut into two pieces and placed in position as shown.

b. A small ball that is rolled onto the inside rim of the plate follows the
    dotted path.

straight line and pushes against the circular rim. The rim exerts an external force (third law) that keeps pushing the ball back toward the center of the plate. As a result, the ball keeps going around in a circle until it passes the end of the rim.

Each time the ball leaves the half-plate, it moves in a straight line in the direction that it was going at that point, in agreement with the first law. The straight line brings it to where the other half of the plate has been set. There, the ball again is forced around the curve. It again exits in a straight line.

When an object moves in a circular path, its direction keeps changing. This is shown in Figure 13, where the direction of each of a series of selected points around the circle is shown by an arrow.

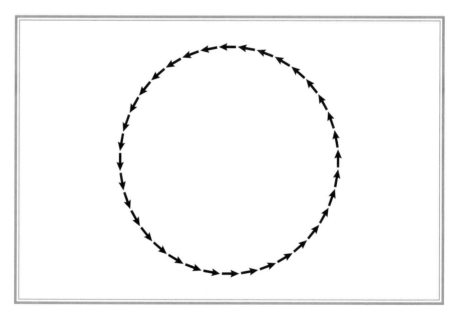

Figure 13. When an object moves in a circle, its direction of motion changes continuously. The arrows show the direction of motion for a series of points on a circle.

Repeat this experiment, but this time tilt the ruler more until one or both of the balls override the slanted rim. What happens after the ball rolls over the barrier?

When the tilt of the ruler is increased, the speed of the ball is increased. A faster ball exerts more force on the rim (second law: $F = ma$). The speed can become great enough that the rim will not have enough force to shove the ball back toward the center. The ball escapes over the rim. When the ball rolls over the rim, it keeps going in a straight line (first law).

Less speed is needed for the golf ball to ride up and over the rim than for the marble. This is because the golf ball weighs more and so can exert a greater force (second law) against the rim. The force that pushes back at an object to keep it from jumping the circular barrier (third law) is called the centripetal force.

A car going around a turn can stay on the road only as long as the force it exerts on the road does not exceed the centripetal force that the road exerts back on it. If the engine of the car makes it go so fast that the tires exert more force than the ground can return, the car will pass from rolling to sliding. It will then skid in a straight line in the direction it was following at that moment.

Road builders can adjust a road that has a sharp turn to allow the car to go at a faster speed without sliding. How is this done?

To allow cars to take turns on a road at a faster speed, engineers make the road banked. This means that the road is tilted at the curve so that it exerts more centripetal force on the car, just the way the slanted rim did in the paper plate experiment. On a banked curve, the outside of the curve is higher than the inside. This helps to oppose the force exerted by the car so that the car can finish the turn. All four turns on the Indy 500 racetrack are banked at just over 9 degrees.

When a car turns right, passengers are "flung" to the left. This is because as the car turns, a rider's upper body keeps going straight ahead. Fortunately, friction and the seat belt hold the body to the seat. Since the car and the person's lower torso are turning right while the upper body is still moving straight ahead, the person feels as if he or she has been shoved left.

Project Ideas and Further Investigations

- What is the best path to take when driving around a corner? Should you go all the way around the outside, cut across it as much as possible, or do something in between? Both Newton and Leibniz (another famous mathematician) studied this problem and mathematically derived an answer. What did they conclude? How do their conclusions stand up under the reality of today's high-speed race cars?

- Use a toy car, a clay figure, and a steel edge or other tool to show what happens to the upper part of the body during a fast turn on a road. Label and explain all the forces involved.

- When there is a thin layer of water on the roadway, as on a rainy day, a car will hydroplane. That is, the car will slide on the layer of water, and it cannot be controlled even at ordinary speed. This happens because the water greatly reduces friction between the tires and the road. How can hydroplaning be avoided? Why is water or oil on the road especially dangerous when driving around a curve? Apply the method of Experiment 3.5 to investigate your hypothesis.

Experiment 3.6

Center of Gravity and Weight Transfer

Materials

* broom
* table
* thick-walled tall narrow plastic glass
* thick-walled short wide plastic glass
* cloth napkin

Braking, accelerating, and cornering all cause a car to act as if weight has been shifted within it. Race car drivers call this phenomenon weight transfer. How can weight appear to be transferred when nothing within the car has moved from its place?

The answer has to do with the fact that the center of gravity of a car is above ground level, whereas frictional forces act at ground level through the contact patch of the tire.

It was Newton who discovered that every object has a spot in it, called the center of gravity, that acts as if all the mass of the object is concentrated there. A sphere has its center of gravity located in its center. For objects of irregular shape, the location of the center of gravity depends on how the mass is distributed.

Obtain a broom and support it on a finger at each end (see Figure 14). Carefully slide your fingers together so that the broom stays balanced horizontally. When your fingers meet under the broom, the center of gravity will be right above them. Is the center of gravity in the center of the entire broom length, at the center of the broomstick, or at another spot?

Place the broom on a table with the bristle end sticking over the end of the table. Gradually slide the bristle end of the stick farther and farther past the edge of the table. At what point does it fall down? Why?

The center of gravity of a broom is closer to the bristle end of the stick than it is to the middle of the handle. All of the broom's mass acts as if it is centered at that point. When an object is in a position where a line drawn vertically down from its center of gravity goes past its base, the object will fall over. So, when you slide the broom past its center of gravity, the broom falls off the table.

The Leaning Tower of Pisa has been able to stay up all these years because its center of gravity has not yet tilted past its base. Similarly, if a person stands upright, her center of gravity is over her feet. If she leans forward until her center of gravity is past her toes, she will fall over (see Figure 15).

Place a tall narrow plastic glass and a short wide plastic glass next to each other on a cloth napkin. Predict what will

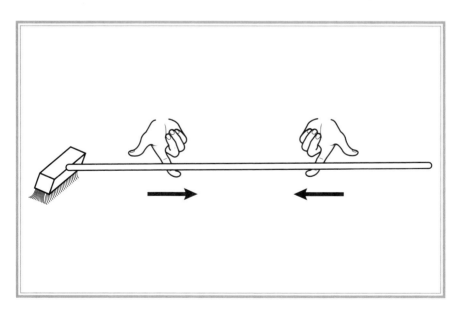

Figure 14. Finding the center of gravity of a broom.

happen to each glass when you pull the napkin sharply toward yourself. Try it. What happens?

You will find that the short wide glass stays in place on the napkin but the tall glass falls backward. When you pull the napkin, your pull acts upon the base of the glass. Friction holds the base of each glass on the napkin so that the glass moves with the napkin. The top of each glass stays where it was, so each glass tilts backward. The high center of gravity of the tall glass tilts past its base. The tall glass falls. The lower center of gravity of the short glass does not move past its base, so it does not fall over. It is the heights at which the forces operate that make the difference. The frictional force is at the base, and the downward force of the glass is at its center of gravity.

Essentially the same thing happens when a race car is braked. The brakes push on the tires and slow them down. The center of gravity of the car is above the ground, and it continues to move on as the car is braked. The downward force exerted by the center of gravity moves forward. The rear end actually becomes lighter while the front end becomes heavier. This temporary shift in weight is an example of weight transfer. As a result of the shift in weight, the ground has to push up harder on the front tires during braking.

Race car drivers know that braking shifts weight to the front of a car and accelerating shifts weight to the rear of the car. Cornering acts to shift weight toward the outside of the curve. Since weight determines friction at every point in the ride, changes in weight affect how the driver must respond. Failure to correctly gauge oversteer may cause the

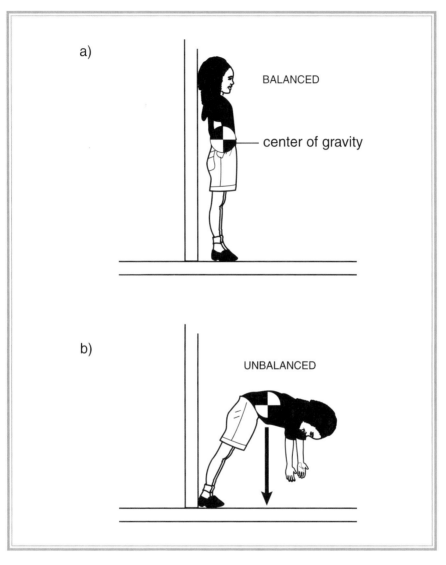

Figure 15. The position of the center of gravity determines whether or not an object falls. If the center of gravity is over the base of the object, the object is balanced. If the center of gravity is over an area outside the base, the object falls over.

a. When the girl shown in the drawing stands upright, her center of gravity is directly above her feet. The girl stands upright.

b. As the girl leans forward more and more, a point is reached where a line drawn down from her center of gravity misses her feet. At that point, the girl will fall over.

rear end to swing out during cornering, throwing the car into a spin. Or, if the front wheels suddenly lose grip going into a curve, the understeer can send the car hurtling toward the outside wall as it moves straight ahead instead of turning.

Project Ideas and Further Investigations

- The weight of a car helps determine how much friction its tires develop, and the friction helps determine the maximum speed the car can safely attain without loss of driver control. What is the effect of weight transfer on the maximum safe speed during cornering or braking? Explain with diagrams.

- What could cause a car in a drag race to have its nose lift off the ground? Explain. Can it really happen?

Experiment 3.7

Down Force

Today, race car designers consider aerodynamics (airflow) to be the most important element in car design. Aerodynamic design involves air resistance (air drag) and down force.

Materials

* * narrow strip of paper
* * small pad of paper
* * scissors
* * sheet of paper, 8½ x 11 in
* * table
* * 6 books

Car designers have to allow for the fact that a bigger engine to help overcome air resistance is heavier. A heavier engine adds to friction, which allows higher speeds to be safely attained without loss of control but also uses up more fuel. Much of the current research on air resistance is carried out by the aerospace industry. It has long been known that as speed doubles, air resistance approximately quadruples. Streamlining helps reduce air resistance. Wind tunnels are used to observe the effects of body design changes.

It is only since about 1980 that the importance of down force has been recognized. The design of the chassis can contribute to the downward pressure of a car on its tires. Increasing the downward pressure on the tires increases friction, which allows the car to go faster without sliding and without loss of driver control. To create down force, the shape of the chassis of a race car is designed to have the opposite effect of airplane wings. The rounded curve at the top of an airplane wing causes airflow to push it upward. If the rounding is at the bottom, the wing, or airfoil, is pushed down.

To simulate an airplane wing, obtain a long strip of paper that is 2 to 3 cm (about 1 in) wide. Place one end into a pad of paper so that it is held securely while the rest of the strip flops down. Hold the pad close to your lips. Blow straight across the top of the paper strip. Does the strip go downward or upward?

If you blow straight across the paper, it moves upward. It was Daniel Bernoulli (1700–1782) who first showed that faster air exerts less pressure than slower air. When you blow air across the top of the strip, this *faster* air above the paper exerts *less* pressure on the strip than the slower air beneath. The slower air beneath pushes the strip upward.

An airplane wing is curved on top and flat on bottom so that the air above it moves faster than below. Hence, the air below pushes it up. To push the chassis of a ground vehicle downward, the bottom of the airfoil is curved and the top is flat.

To demonstrate what happens when the faster flow of air is below a surface, cut an 8½-by-11-in sheet of paper in half. On a table or desk, bridge two piles of three books each with the half sheet of paper. Bend down and blow horizontally under the paper. Does the paper move up or down?

You can expect to see the sheet of paper sag downward. You have created down force because the pressure on the paper is greater on the side where the airflow is slower.

In 1980, the first auto undercarriage shaped like a tunnel was developed to create low pressure under the bottom of a race car. Today, this feature is standard in race cars. At top speeds, Indy 500 cars can produce three times the weight of the car in down force. There are also devices used on race cars today that reduce disturbance of airflow under the car.

Neither Newton nor Galileo ever made or saw devices in action on Earth's surface that operated without friction. Even so, Galileo was able to perceive the first law of motion and Newton was able to develop the three laws with a complete concept of force and how it operated. These accomplishments were surely close to miraculous.

Project Ideas and Further Investigations

- The devices currently in use to produce down force on race cars include front air dams, rear spoilers, strakes, plates, and side skirts. Find out what these devices are. Develop demonstrations to show how one or more of these work.
- Construct a diagram to show where each of the devices listed above is placed on the car, what it looks like, and how it works. Look up and list other such devices with their function and placement.
- Make a simple wind tunnel to examine aerodynamic properties of toy cars with emphasis on streamlining and down force. Several medium-sized cardboard boxes can be taped together for the wind tunnel. A fan or the hose of a vacuum cleaner attached to the vent outlet can be used to supply wind. Some fans allow different airspeeds.

Chapter 4

Newton in Outer Space

Enveloped in flames over the launchpad, the huge vehicle lifts majestically off the ground. Slowly, then accelerating, it rises into the sky on a fiery tail. Below, it leaves a long, smoky white trail. Soon it is only a dot. Then it is gone into the heavens.

Another vehicle has been sent into the skies, perhaps to dock with the International Space Station, to repair the Hubble Space Telescope in orbit, to loft artificial satellites, to land on the Moon or on Mars, to look at Venus, Jupiter, or Saturn, or to go out into the universe.

Did Newton foresee this? Perhaps he did. He opened the door to all of the above when he stated the three laws of motion, mathematically described how gravity works, calculated the speed needed to get an object to go into orbit around Earth, showed what the shape of the orbit would be, and explained why the Moon circles Earth without falling into it.

Experiment 4.1

Air Resistance

Air exerts a force that opposes the motion of any object moving in it. This opposing force is called air drag or air resistance. As the object barrels through the air, it encounters more impacts from the molecules in front than in back of it, causing it to be slowed.

Materials

* 2 sheets of paper
* book
* plastic drinking cup
* flat piece of metal
* water
* sink

To see the effect of air drag, crumple a sheet of paper into a ball. Drop the ball from shoulder height. Take an identical sheet of paper, uncrumpled, and drop it in the same way. Do they fall at the same speed?

The crumpled paper ball drops quickly straight down.

The uncrumpled sheet falls much less rapidly than the paper ball because the sheet presents a much larger surface to the moving air molecules than does the crumpled paper ball.

Hold a book horizontally a few feet above a surface. Allow it to drop. Pick it up and place the uncrumpled sheet of paper on top of the book. Hold the book with the paper on it horizontally above the surface as before and allow them both to drop. Does the paper float down or fall quickly?

This time, the paper falls at the same rate as the book. The book protects the paper from the air molecules.

Here is a different experiment. Obtain a plastic drinking cup and a piece of flat metal large enough to cover the mouth of the cup. The back of a metal tray, pan, or cookie sheet could be used. Run several inches of water into a sink. Hold the cup high up over the sink, turn it over, and observe it as it falls mouth down into the sink. Next, fill the cup with water, wet the metal sheet, and place the metal sheet on top of the cup. Hold the metal sheet tightly over the cup while you turn them over together over the sink. Let go of the cup and pull the sheet sharply out from under the cup (see Figure 16), similarly to the way a tablecloth is pulled out from under a set of dishes in that old trick. Does the water drop straight down from the cup while the cup floats down?

Both the cup and the water should drop together into the sink. The water protects the cup from the air molecules.

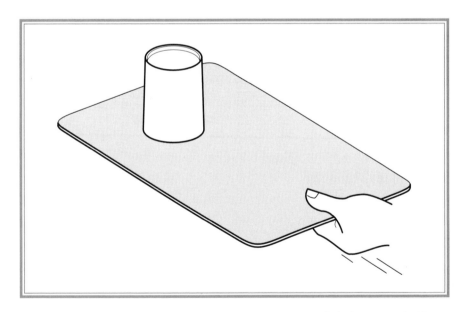

Figure 16. A metal sheet with an inverted paper cup full of water is held over a sink. When the sheet is yanked out from under the cup, the cup and the water will fall downward. Does the water spill out while the paper cup floats down, or do they fall together?

In the absence of air resistance, all objects fall to the ground due to gravity with the same acceleration. Near Earth's surface, objects fall 9.8 m/s faster every second (32 ft/s each second).

Project Ideas and Further Investigations

- Obtain different balls—baseball, Ping-Pong ball, tennis ball, golf ball, etc. Drop them from four feet high and then, **under adult supervision**, from ten feet high, measuring the time it takes each to hit the ground. Make a chart of the results. Compare and explain.

- What causes a kite to stay up? What causes it to fall? How fast does it fall? Construct a kite shaped like a parachute. Can you get it to fly? How? Does it stay up by itself? Explain your observations.

- Look up the topic of terminal velocity. Construct several different parachutes to test which design reaches terminal velocity the soonest when dropped. Develop a hypothesis to explain why.

Experiment 4.2

Compound Motion

Watch a basketball player dribbling a ball while running. Does the player slap the ball down or forward? Try it yourself.

A basketball player dribbles the ball by slapping it down, not forward, when running at a steady speed. The ball will move forward with the player and be alongside for the next slap. This agrees with Newton's first law. Both the player and the ball are moving forward. As the ball drops, it continues to move forward at the same speed as the player does. When a ball falls down and moves ahead at the same time, it is showing compound motion.

Based on this, which do you think will hit the ground first, a coin that falls straight down or one that is flung straight out from the same height?

To find out, place a ruler on a table and place the two coins as shown in Figure 17. When you strike the edge of the ruler sharply where indicated by the arrow on the diagram, the coin it hits is flung straight out. At the same time, the other coin will drop straight down. Listen after you strike the edge of the ruler to hear which coin hits the ground first.

You should hear both coins strike the ground at the same time, even though one was flung out horizontally. Evidently, the coin hit by the ruler keeps traveling horizontally even while is it moving downward. It undergoes compound motion.

Repeat the experiment but try launching the coins with less force than before, and then with more force. What differences do you observe?

You will find that the coin dropped vertically always lands in the same spot. The less the force with which you horizontally launch the other coin, the closer it lands to the dropped one.

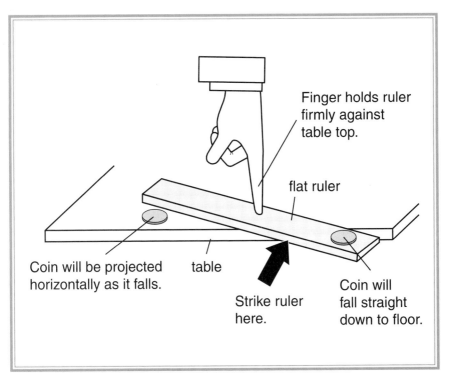

Figure 17. By striking the ruler at the place shown, two identical coins will be dropped simultaneously so that one falls straight down while the other is flung outward. Differences in the times of fall of the two coins may be observed by listening to the sound of their impacts when they hit the ground.

To observe the approximate path that the coin launched horizontally follows, adjust the end of the nozzle of a hose to give a narrow stream of water. Shoot it straight out horizontally and observe the path. Draw a picture of it.

Project Idea and Further Investigation

Devise an experiment to show in detail the path that a small, hard, round object takes when propelled horizontally into the air. **Carry out this experiment under adult supervision**. Be sure that nothing is in the path of the object you are launching. What happens to this path when the horizontal force is increased? What happens to this path when the height of release is increased? Explain the path in terms of compound motion.

Experiment 4.3

Why Doesn't the Moon Fall Down to Earth?

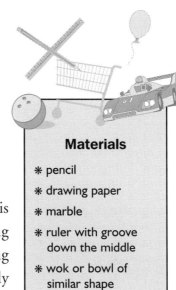

Materials

* pencil
* drawing paper
* marble
* ruler with groove down the middle
* wok or bowl of similar shape

It is said that Newton developed his law of gravitation while sitting under an apple tree and observing an apple fall. If Newton had really watched the apple fall, he would have known, based on his own laws of motion, that the apple had to have a force acting upon it because it speeded up as it dropped. According to his laws of motion, acceleration occurs only with an unbalanced force. Newton may have conjectured, therefore, that an invisible force was pulling the apple down. How high up could the invisible force be felt? Maybe all the way to the Moon. Maybe throughout the universe. From that observation, perhaps, came the law of universal gravitation.

This law says that all masses attract each other. They do so in proportion to their mass. The attraction decreases rapidly as the distance between the masses widens. Newton stated the law as an exact mathematical equation.

Newton carried out calculations on the orbit of the Moon based on his law of gravitation. His calculations agreed with the known facts about the Moon's orbit. Evidently, it was an invisible force, which Newton called gravity, that was pulling the Moon around Earth.

Newton proposed a thought experiment. It involved firing a cannonball from a cannon. Picture a very high mountain. It is so high up that it is above most of the air in our atmosphere, so that friction will not interfere. In your imagination, fire a cannonball horizontally out from a cannon at the top of that mountain. Based on Experiment 4.2, what do you predict will be the path of the cannonball?

Did you predict that the cannonball would arc downward? It would move with compound motion outward (first law of motion) and downward (law of universal gravitation). It will keep falling in an arc until it crashes into Earth. That is the most likely scenario.

Now imagine that you load more gunpowder into the cannon and fire the cannonball out faster. What happens this time?

You can expect the cannonball to travel farther before it crashes.

Suppose you keep increasing the charge in the cannon until the ball goes so far out that it misses Earth altogether when it falls.

Draw a picture of this. What will be the path of the falling cannonball as it misses Earth and continues? Remember that Earth is still attracting the ball. Add this to your picture.

See Figure 18 for a diagram similar to one that Newton drew of the trajectory of the cannonball when fired at different speeds. Newton published his diagram of the cannonball's motion in 1687. It showed that when the ball goes fast enough, it keeps falling toward Earth but keeps passing Earth as it falls. Recall in Experiment 3.5 how the rim of the plate kept forcing the ball into circular motion. In that experiment, the ball would have kept going in a straight line were it not for the force from the rim. A similar process occurs here. The cannonball would fall past Earth and keep going into outer space were it not for Earth's gravitational pull. It is this gravitational attraction that keeps forcing the ball into a circular path. The imaginary cannonball would keep going around Earth forever, a cannonball in orbit.

The same idea explains why the Moon doesn't fall down to Earth. The Moon travels fast enough to keep passing Earth but not fast enough to escape from Earth's gravitational attraction. The Moon is always falling toward Earth and is always missing it.

Newton could never carry out his experiment. He would have needed a mountain 200 miles high, much higher than any on Earth, and he would have needed a cannon with firepower more than four times greater than any cannon that has ever been fired.

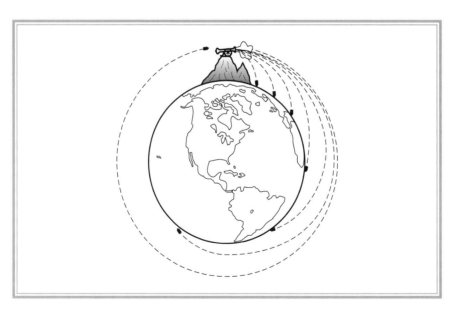

Figure 18. Newton's cannonball thought experiment.

You can simulate how the speed with which an object is fired from Newton's imaginary cannon determines whether the object goes into orbit or falls to the ground. Do this by allowing a marble to roll down a grooved ruler held horizontally to the inside of the top edge of a wok or similarly shaped bowl. Adjust the slant of the ruler so that the marble rolls around the inside of the rim. Then launch the marble at different speeds (slant the ruler both more and then less than the first launch). Observe the path of the marble each time.

When launched too slowly, the ball will roll down into the center of the bowl. When launched fast enough, it will circle around the edge of the wok. Friction will slow it enough so that gravity eventually pulls it down. It will gradually spiral to the bottom of the wok.

Experiment 4.4

"5 . . . 4 . . . 3 . . . 2 . . . 1 . . . Ignition! We Have Liftoff!"

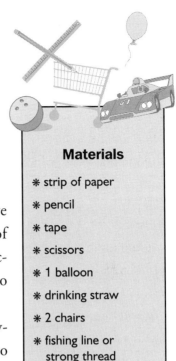

What causes a rocket to move upward? Newton's third law of motion, the law of action and reaction, is what makes it possible to send a rocket skyward.

Exactly the same law that governs the ascent of a rocket applies to this experiment, in which you will make a balloon "rocket." A fishing line running through a straw will be

Materials

∗ strip of paper

∗ pencil

∗ tape

∗ scissors

∗ 1 balloon

∗ drinking straw

∗ 2 chairs

∗ fishing line or strong thread several meters (yards) long

strung tightly between two chairs. The balloon will be taped to the straw. When the balloon "blasts off," it will have to travel along the fishing line.

You will need a nozzle for the balloon rocket. Start by wrapping a short strip of paper around a pencil. Tape the end to form a short paper tube and pull it off the pencil. Cut the paper tube to about 1.5 cm (about ½ in) long. Slip this tube into the neck of a balloon and tape it firmly in place so that it is 2 to 4 cm (at least 1 in) below the opening. Blow up the balloon and knot or tie it so that the tube is inside the closed neck.

Attach a drinking straw to the outside of the inflated balloon with strips of tape, as shown in Figure 19.

Set up two chairs 2 to 3 meters (2 to 3 yards) apart. Cut a piece of fishing line or strong thread long enough to stretch well past the two chairs. Thread the line through the straw. Tie the line from one chair just below the seat to the other chair at the same height so that the line is tightly stretched.

Pull the balloon along the fishing line so that its neck is at one chair. What, if anything, happens to it? Cut off the knotted end of the balloon just above the nozzle. What happens this time? How is this explained by Newton's third law? What is acting and what is reacting?

When you push the balloon over to one chair, it stays there. When the knot is cut, the balloon shoots along the line toward the other chair. It may look to you as if the air coming out is pushing in one direction so that the balloon simply moves in the other direction. This is not quite why the balloon obeys Newton's third law. Inside the balloon, air molecules are in constant motion, bouncing all over and

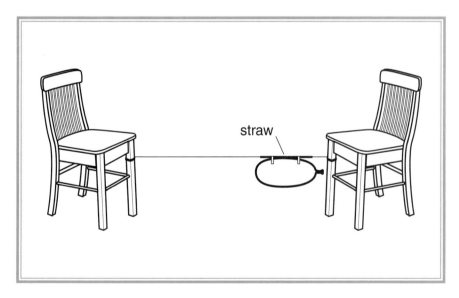

Figure 19. Newton's third law of motion is illustrated by a balloon filled with air. When air jets out of the balloon in one direction, the balloon travels in the opposite direction.

banging all around inside the skin. There is only one portion of the skin against which they cannot push. That place is where molecules can exit through the neck of the balloon. As a result, the push of the air molecules all around the inside of the balloon is balanced except for the spot where the air exits. Opposite that opening, the unbalanced force of the air molecules pushes the balloon forward, as illustrated in Figure 20.

A rocket is similarly launched into space by violently heated gases that surge against the rocket chamber and out through the opening in the tail. The thrust of the gases in the chamber is unbalanced due to the gases exiting through the opening. The unbalanced force causes the rocket to soar upward. The proof that the propellant force is not due to the gases pushing against the outside air is that a rocket works in airless space.

Once an artificial satellite is in orbit, no fuel is needed to keep it going. It obeys Newton's first law and keeps coasting ahead while falling around Earth in the same way that the Moon does.

What happens to a rocket that is launched to reach a speed greater than the 28,000 km/hr (17,500 mph) needed to get into circular orbit? The faster the rocket goes, the higher its orbit. As the rocket goes higher in orbit, Earth's pull on it decreases. This is because the gravitational attraction between any two objects decreases the father apart they are. If the rocket can be launched with enough velocity, Earth will be unable to pull it into orbit. When that happens, the rocket will completely escape from Earth and travel to outer space. The escape velocity of a rocket from Earth's surface is 40,250 km/hr (25,000 mph), ignoring air friction. See Figure 21.

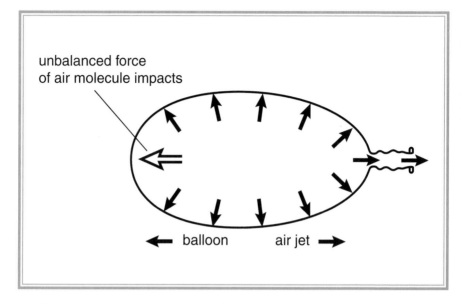

unbalanced force
of air molecule impacts

← balloon   air jet →

Figure 20. This figure shows what happens when the nozzle of an inflated balloon is opened. Before the nozzle was opened, air molecules inside the balloon were beating equally on all sides of the balloon, as indicated by the arrows. The forces exerted on the walls of the balloon by all the air molecules were balanced. When the nozzle of the balloon is opened, air jets out the opening. As a result, the force of the air molecules is no longer balanced. The unbalanced force pushes the balloon in the direction opposite to the exiting air jet.

When a spacecraft or artificial satellite orbits Earth, it encounters scattered molecules of gas that gradually slow it down. As the spacecraft slows down, its orbit becomes lower and lower until it encounters enough atmosphere to send it plunging to Earth.

A spacecraft returning to land on Earth must first be carefully slowed down by firing its rockets. As the craft slows down, its orbit becomes lower until it zings through Earth's atmosphere. Friction, acting as an atmospheric brake, slows the craft until it can be landed safely. Tremendous heat can be produced during reentry into the atmosphere, so the nose of the craft has to be protected from burning up by special tiles. To help reduce the friction to a safe level, the vehicle enters the atmosphere at a small angle to it.

On March 23, 2001, the fifteen-year-old failing Russian space station, *Mir,* was deliberately brought down from space in such a way as to be safely destroyed during the reentry process. *Mir* was deorbited with the aid of braking thrusters until it was on a planned path through the atmosphere. Most of it burned up as it zinged back down. The fiery remains of the craft, as planned, plunged into a remote area of the South Pacific Ocean.

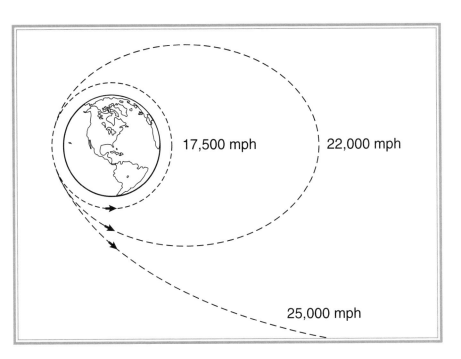

Figure 21. Path of a rocket after launching from Earth at different speeds. At the escape velocity, 25,000 miles per hour, the rocket will shoot off into outer space.

Project Ideas and Further Investigations

- How does the size of the tail opening affect the speed of a rocket? What is your hypothesis? Repeat the experiment with the rocket balloon of Experiment 4.4 but make changes in the size of the tube in the neck of the balloon. Chart your results and explain them.

- What do you predict would happen if a bigger balloon were used for Experiment 4.4? Find out. Explain your results.

- Does the shape of the balloon make a difference in Experiment 4.4? To find out, use two balloons with different shapes but with the same volume. Explain your results.

- How is the thrust of a real rocket engine controlled by the shape of the gas expansion chamber?

- Can the distance traveled by the rocket balloon of Experiment 4.4 be increased by streamlining? Find out by making a nose cone for the balloon.

- Can you launch a rocket balloon vertically upward on a string? Try tying a string from the ground up a flagpole to use for the upward track for the balloon. How far can you get the balloon to go? What modifications can you introduce to get the balloon to go higher? How well do they work? Suppose you hang on the balloon a small paper cup with a paper clip in it. Can you still get the balloon to rise up the string? How many paper clips can the balloon support before it can no longer rise? Note that at that point the balloon is like a rocket that is too heavy for its engine to lift off the ground.

- Carry out three launchings of a balloon on a string, one horizontally as in Experiment 4.4, one vertically, and one at an angle. Compare the results and explain them.
- Simple rockets can be made from paper tubes. Form a tube by rolling a paper strip around a pencil and taping the end in place, then freeing the pencil. The upper end of the tube should be taped shut. Fins need to be attached to the lower end of the tube or it will wobble in flight and then fall. You will need to experiment to find the best shapes, locations, and numbers of fins. To launch the rocket, you can simply blow through a straw into the bottom end. You could also consider more powerful sources of propelled air. How does your paper rocket illustrate Newton's third law? List the variables that you altered during this experiment, and explain the outcomes. What was the farthest your rocket went? What design made this possible? Why was it effective? **In all rocket tests, be sure that there is no person or object close enough to be harmed by the launch or the rocket**.
- How do tail fins affect the performance of the rocket balloon of Experiment 4.4?
- Design, construct, and test a more effective rocket than the balloon rocket of Experiment 4.4. Small rockets may be launched using gases produced from a chemical reaction. A safe reaction that produces carbon dioxide as a propellant is a mixture of vinegar and baking soda. Measure how high up the rocket goes. Describe additional

improvements and the results of testing. **All rocket experiments must be done with adult supervision.**

- Build models of actual rockets that have been launched into space using easily available scrap materials such as cardboard tubes, spools, and Styrofoam. Prepare an information sheet for each rocket that you construct, describing the original designer of the rocket, the time period when the rocket was designed, and the rocket's special characteristics.

- What is a two-stage rocket? What is the purpose of the stages? Draw a diagram of a rocket with two or more stages. How much more effective is it than a rocket without stages?

Experiment 4.5
G Forces

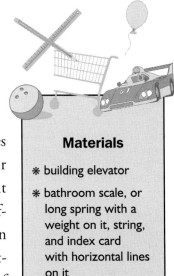

When a rocket is launched, it pushes the astronauts, strapped into their seats, with such force that different parts of their bodies are affected differently. Photographs have shown the face of an astronaut partly flattened during the short period of tremendous acceleration. Astronauts

endure 3 g's during a launch in the space shuttle, although other launches have caused as much as 6 g's. One g force produces the ordinary acceleration due to gravity, 9.8 m/s^2 (32 ft/s^2).

The effect of upward acceleration can be observed in an elevator. A sensitive spring bathroom scale, the kind that has a pointer that whips around the dial to get your weight, is best for this. Stand on the scale while the elevator ascends. Watch it at the beginning of the ride and then as the elevator slows to a stop.

You can instead hang a long spring from the top of the elevator with a weight at the end. Hang an index card with horizontal lines on it from the ceiling so that it is visible behind the weight. The card will enable you to tell when the weight moves vertically. Observe what happens to the weight as the elevator moves.

You will be able to see that your weight or that the weight on the spring appears to increase very slightly as the elevator starts upward. It decreases very slightly as the elevator slows to a stop.

Observe the scale or the weight as the elevator goes back down for a preview to the next experiment.

Experiment 4.6

Weightlessness

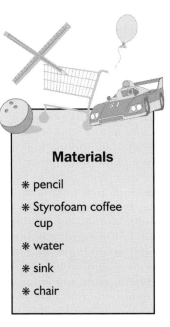

Once astronauts are in orbit, they float inside the orbiter along with everything else that is not fastened down. There is no up or down inside. In order to direct their motion during a task outside the spacecraft, an astronaut has to use small thrusters on a space pack.

Materials

* pencil
* Styrofoam coffee cup
* water
* sink
* chair

Actually, the astronauts, at 200 miles up, are still well within Earth's gravitational field and are not completely weightless. The gravitational force at that height is about 90 percent of what it is on Earth. Instead, the astronauts are falling all the time, in the same way that the Moon falls around Earth. However, all the objects in the space vessel, and the vessel itself, are falling together, so they all seem to float together.

To show a similar effect, use a pencil to punch a hole near the bottom of a Styrofoam cup. Cover the hole with a finger while filling the cup with water. Holding the cup over a sink, remove your finger from the cup. What happens?

Again cover the hole with your finger and refill the cup. Carry out the rest of this experiment outdoors. Throw the cup straight up and observe. If you have trouble getting it to go straight up, stand on a chair and drop it straight down.

When you hold the cup over the sink and remove your finger, water flows freely through the hole. When you throw the cup straight up, the water stops coming out on the way up and as it falls. This is because both the cup and the water are rising or falling with the same acceleration due to your throw and then to gravity. Compared to each other, the cup and the water are weightless. If a cup of water (no hole in it) were sitting on a scale and you tossed the scale upward with the cup on it, they would similarly fall together so that the scale would read zero. They would be in free fall.

You experience free fall on a swing when it reaches the top of the arc and is about to change direction. At that moment, you and the seat of the swing are weightless. You can get a similar feeling at the top of a roller coaster as it first starts to descend.

Weightlessness in space is called microgravity. Astronauts undergo a variety of possible changes while in a microgravity environment. When gravity no longer acts to pull body fluids downward, there is a shift in body fluids from the lower to upper parts of the body. Extended stays may cause a loss of muscle tone, a decrease in production of red blood cells, and an increase in production of white blood cells. Fortunately, most of these effects reverse upon returning to Earth. The astronauts do exercises and ingest a diet designed to minimize these effects.

Project Ideas and Further Investigations

- Construct a simulated space capsule. Place within it labeled mock-ups of all the instruments needed to successfully operate the craft. Show the calibration and units for each. Where is each one best located? Why? What facilities are needed for the astronauts to conduct the activities needed for daily living? How are these constructed and where are they placed? How do the astronauts operate the thrusters and the door to the spacecraft? What kind of help does an astronaut need to get into a space suit while inside the capsule? What tools must be supplied for everyday activities and for emergencies? You may wish to do this project with partners or with your class at school.

- Construct a device to record the reading on a scale of an object in free fall. One suggestion for this is to use a small postal scale anchored to a small board. A weight can be sealed onto the platform of the scale. The board can be suspended high up on a rope wound around a pulley. A large piece of foam may be placed underneath to cushion the landing of the board. When the rope is released, the board will fall straight down. A video camera or other photographic device may be placed to record the reading on the postal scale as it descends. Explain the reading.

Even though Isaac Newton lived over three hundred years ago, his discoveries are still affecting our daily lives and leading to new knowledge. Recognition of his importance was shown by the Apollo astronauts as they sped through space to the Moon. They sent the following message by radio to Mission Control: "We would like to thank the person who made this trip possible, Sir Isaac Newton."

Appendix A

Answers to Questions on Page 7

Question	Where answer may be found
Why do automobile wheels spin without gripping when a car makes too fast a start?	Experiment 3.4
If you need a seat belt because you are slammed forward, why do you need a headrest?	Experiment 3.2
Why do some of the groceries in a shopping cart slide forward when the cart is jerked to a halt?	Experiment 2.1
What makes a bowling ball curve sharply only when it gets near the pins?	Experiment 1.2
If you push on a building, does it push on you?	Experiment 2.7
Why doesn't the Moon fall down to Earth?	Experiment 4.3
When a horse balks at a fence, refusing to go over it, what happens to the rider?	Experiment 3.1 (A rider on a balking horse is like a passenger in a car that is braked sharply.)

Further Reading

Adams, Richard, and Robert Gardner. *Ideas for Science Projects.* Revised edition. New York: Franklin Watts, 1998.

Anderson, Margaret Jean. *Isaac Newton: The Greatest Scientist of All Time.* Springfield, N.J.: Enslow Publishers, Inc., 1996.

Bloomfield, Louis A. *How Things Work.* New York: John Wiley & Sons, Inc., 1997.

de Pinna, Simon. *Forces and Motion.* Austin, Tex.: Steck-Vaughn Company, 1998.

The DK Science Encyclopedia. Revised edition. New York: DK Publishing, Inc., 1998.

Ehrlich, Robert. *Turning the World Inside Out and 174 Other Simple Physics Demonstrations.* Princeton, N.J.: Princeton University Press, 1990.

Friedhoffer, Robert, Richard Kaufman, and Linda Eisenberg. *Forces, Motion and Energy.* New York: Franklin Watts, 1992.

Gardner, Robert. *Experiments with Motion.* Springfield, N.J.: Enslow Publishers, Inc., 1995.

———. *Science Projects About Physics in the Home.* Berkeley Heights, N.J.: Enslow Publishers, 1999.

Gilbert, Harry, and Diana Gilbert Smith. *Gravity, the Glue of the Universe: History and Activities.* Englewood, Colo.: Teacher Ideas Press, div. of Libraries Unlimited, Inc., 1997.

Hewitt, Paul G. *Conceptual Physical Science.* Second edition. Menlo Park, Calif.: Addison Wesley Longman, Inc., 1999.

Lafferty, Peter. *Eyewitness: Force and Motion.* New York: DK Publishing, Inc., 1992.

Internet Addresses

Trinity College, Dublin. *Mathematicians of the Seventeenth and Eighteenth Centuries.* "Sir Isaac Newton (1624–1727)." <www.maths.tcd.ie/pub/HistMath/People/Newton/Rouse Ball/RB_Newton.html>.

Cislunar Aerospace, Inc. *Aerodynamics and Automobile Racing.* © 1997. <http://wings.avkids.com/Book/Sports/instructor/race_car-01.html>.

California Institute of Technology. *The Space Place.* © 2001. <http://spaceplace.jpl.nasa.gov/rocket.htm>.

Index

About the Author

Madeline Goodstein is a retired professor of chemistry from Central Connecticut State University. In her spare time she enjoys spending time with her family and friends, as well as writing, reading, and running.